WHAT MAKES
HIGH-
PERFORMING
BOARDS

Effective governance practices in member-serving organizations

BETH GAZLEY, PhD and ASHLEY BOWERS

★**asae**
association
management
press·

WASHINGTON, DC

The authors have worked diligently to ensure that all information in this book is accurate as of the time of publication and consistent with standards of good practice in the general management community. As research and practice advance, however, standards may change. For this reason it is recommended that readers evaluate the applicability of any recommendations in light of particular situations and changing standards.

ASAE: The Center for Association Leadership
Association Management Press
1575 I Street, NW
Washington, DC 20005-1103
Phone: (202) 626-2723; (888) 950-2723 outside the metropolitan Washington, DC area
Fax: (202) 220-6439
Email: books@asaecenter.org
We connect great ideas and great people to inspire leadership and achievement in the association community.

Keith C. Skillman, CAE, Vice President, Publications,
    ASAE: The Center for Association Leadership
Baron Williams, CAE, Director of Book Publishing,
    ASAE: The Center for Association Leadership
Cover and interior by Troy Scott Parker, Cimarron Design, cimarrondesign.com

This book is available at a special discount when ordered in bulk quantities. For information, contact the ASAE Member Service Center at (202) 371-0940.

A complete catalog of titles is available on the ASAE website at www.asaecenter.org.

ISBN-13: 978-0-88034-368-8
ISBN-10: 0-88034-368-0

Printed in the United States of America.

10 9 8 7 6 5 4 3 2 1

Table of Contents

Table of Figures   v
Acknowledgements   vii

Introduction and Key Findings   1

CHAPTER ONE
The Challenge of Good Governance: Some Background   8

CHAPTER TWO
A Snapshot of the Association Environment   16

CHAPTER THREE
Board Size, Structure, and Selection   28

CHAPTER FOUR
Board Operating Norms and Decision Making   50

CHAPTER FIVE
"Good Governance" Practices in Member-Serving Organizations   62

CHAPTER SIX
How Do CEOs Rate Their Board's Performance?   76

CHAPTER SEVEN
Benchmarking "Good Governance"   99

APPENDIX A
Methodology   103

About the Authors   107
Bibliography   109

Table of Figures

1.1 A "Systems" View of Boards   12

2.1 CEO Training and Experience   16

2.2 CEO Turnover   17

2.3 Responding Organizations   18

2.4 Organizational Membership   19

2.5 Organizational Purpose   20

2.6 Tax Status   20

2.7 Membership Work Sectors   21

2.8 Geographic Scope of Membership   22

2.9 Organization's Overall Pattern of Membership Growth   23

2.10 Organization's Overall Pattern of Budget Growth   23

2.11 Cross-Tabulation of Membership and Budget Growth   24

2.12 Level of Competition for Members Between Organizations Serving This Field or Industry   24

2.13 Organizational Staffing   25

2.14 Number of Organizational Staff (in FTEs)   26

2.15 Turnover Rate Among Key Staff   26

2.16 Relationship Between Rate of Staff Turnover (Horizontal) and Staffing Structure (Vertical)   27

3.1 Number of Voting Board Members   31

3.2 Formal Diversity Goals, Restrictions, or Requirements for Board Members   33

3.3 Board Member Nominations   35

3.4 Board Member Election Process   37

3.5 Board Election Competitiveness   38

3.6 Difficulty in Finding Qualified People to Serve as Board Member   39

3.7 Qualifications Sought by Respondents Reporting Difficulty in Finding Qualified Board Members   39

3.8   CEO's Role on the Board   42

3.9   Percentage of Organizations That Have Policies Specifying Board Member Term Lengths   43

3.10   Board Member Term Limits   44

3.11   Turnover Rate Among Board Members   45

3.12   Comparing Rates of Staff and Board Turnover   45

3.13   Comparing CEO Assessments of Board Turnover Rate Against Association Policy on Term Limits   46

4.1   Frequency of Board Meetings   52

4.2   Frequency of Unanimous Board Votes   57

4.3   Board Task Assignments   58

4.4   Time Usage During Board Meetings   59

4.5   Level of Organizational Strategic Activity   60

5.1   Method for Documenting, Tracking, or Reporting Representational Goals and Requirements   65

5.2   Organizational Achievement of Representational Goals and Requirements   65

5.3   Use of Board Development or Training Resources   70

5.4   Board Self-Evaluation Process   71

5.5   Goals Used for Board Self-Assessments   71

5.6   CEO and Staff Time Spent Supporting the Board   74

6.1   Quality of Board Relationships with Stakeholders   79

6.2   Measurement of Board Performance, Activities Rated Most Positively   80

6.3   Measurement of Board Performance, Activities That Need Improvement   81

6.4   Dimensions of Board Performance   82

6.5   Environmental Factors: Board Performance Related to External Dynamics   84

6.6   Structural Factors: Board Performance Related to Board Size, Selection, and Structure   86

6.7   Management Quality: Board Performance Related to CEO Characteristics   88

6.8   Staff Capacity: Board Performance Related to Staffing Characteristics   92

6.9   Board Performance and Strategic Orientation   93

6.10   The Board and a Culture of Learning: Board Performance Related to Board Development, Training, and Self-Assessment   96

Acknowledgements

Special thanks for their contributions to the study design and report to ASAE Foundation Research Committee members Hannes Combest, CAE; Mark Engle, CAE; Greg Fine, CAE; Chris Mahaffey, CAE; and Marsha Rhea, CAE; ASAE Past Board Chairman Peter O'Neil, CAE; ASAE CEO John H. Graham IV, CAE; ASAE Executive Vice President and ASAE Foundation President Susan Robertson, CAE; ASAE staff Chelsea Killam; Sharon Moss, CAE; and Keith Skillman, CAE; and consultants Katha Kissman and Francie Ostrower.

Introduction and Key Findings

ASSOCIATIONS AND ORGANIZATIONS WITH dues-paying members serve a broad swath of society, ranging from professional and occupational societies, to trade associations, to arts and cultural institutions, labor unions, producers' cooperatives, sports and recreational clubs, chambers of commerce, social and fraternal clubs, and academic and learned societies. They haven't been studied nearly as much as charities have. But they are also led by boards, and good governance matters equally to them.

For these organizations, this study offers a solution to the anecdotes and conventional wisdom that dominate the discussion of good governance. In other words, we're about to demonstrate that good governance relies on a lot more than board size. For our readers interested in benchmarking, we begin by testing the frequency and variation of recommended practices across different kinds of organizations. Where mission, size, or tax status matters, we report it—but don't expect these organizational features to matter as much as you would expect. Instead, we go further by using analytic techniques (presented in a clear and understandable way) to identify the good governance practices that matter regardless of differences in organizational size, staffing, tax status, and other circumstances. The results will help you understand patterns of related behaviors within organizations that support high board performance and that are intentional and not dependent on sector or capacity.

Basis for our results and key findings

The results come from a survey of 1,585 nonprofit CEOs and executive directors fielded by Indiana University and the ASAE Foundation between November 2012 and February 2013. Using ASAE members and a stratified random sample of nonmembers, we produce a generalizable study of board practices in U.S.-based nonprofit organizations of any tax status that serve a membership (results are limited to organizations that file a 990 information return, and those with at least one paid staff member; margin of error: 2–3 percent).

For each member-serving organization, the chief staff person (referred to herein as "CEO") answered questions addressing the organizational environment, board structure, board selection procedures and challenges, the deliberative processes and the governance models they employ, board relations with staff, members, chapters, and other stakeholders, board development and self-assessment practices, and CEO assessments of board performance. Corresponding financial data drawn directly from IRS 990 forms was added later so that we could compare organizations based on budget size.

The details follow in the next six chapters, but here are our key findings:

The diversity of the association sector means there will be no single recipe for a high-performing board.

The member-serving sector is large, diverse, and complex. Governance practices will reflect this diversity. The competitiveness of an organization's environment, its geographic scope, complexity, and budget dynamics influence not just board size and structure, but also a board's ability to recruit the members it needs and secure the stable staffing on which boards depend.

Tax status, age, and membership structure shape boards in important ways.

For example, while half of 501(c)(3) charities and 501(c)(6) business leagues do not hold competitive elections, most 501(c)(5) labor organizations do, as do most chapter-based organizations. Labor organizations are four times as likely as business leagues to allow the CEO a vote on the board. Younger organizations have higher staff and board turnover, but also more upward growth in membership and budget.

Board recruitment is still a challenge.

As other studies have also found, most CEOs report difficulty in finding qualified board members. Qualities most in demand are time availability, strategic thinking and leadership skills, fundraising or giving abilities, and an interest in the organization's mission. Rather than posing a recruitment problem for boards, term limits appear to support healthy board turnover.

Many boards put a limited emphasis on performance measurement.

While the majority of member-serving boards follow some or all of the governance practices recommended in the expert literature, we found plenty of gaps. Half of boards do not set performance goals for themselves or assess their own performance. One in six boards allows direct appointments by affiliated organizations, a practice we find connected to other board dysfunctions. One in five boards does not evaluate the CEO and staff who report directly to the board.

High-performing boards have a strong strategic focus.

More than half of member-serving boards spend at least 25 percent of their meeting time on strategic thinking and discussion, and two thirds work jointly with staff to develop a strategic plan. This strategic focus pays off in higher CEO ratings across nearly all of our performance measures.

Many high-performing boards are associated with growing organizations.

Boards serving organizations with growing membership or budget numbers were consistently rated higher on most performance measures. While we would need more information to understand whether CEOs are simply rewarding boards of healthier organizations with better ratings, or whether healthy boards can claim the credit for the growth, the connection between strong boards and organizational performance is clear.

CEO ratings reflect the value of training staff in board support.

Professional training of staff supports board performance. For example, organizations with staff who are ASAE members were considerably more likely than non-ASAE members to use board development tools. More staff time spent on board support decreased the number of reported board problems, such as the absence of a quorum at a meeting or the premature departure of a board member.

CEO ratings reflect the value of investing in board development and training.

Board training and development was strongly associated with higher board performance.

Staff turnover is linked to poor performing boards.

Nearly half of our respondents were planning to leave their position (29 percent in the next three years). CEOs planning to leave the organization were highly dissatisfied with board performance.

Board size matters some, but board focus matters most.

Refuting some of the conventional wisdom about big boards versus small boards, we found that larger boards were more likely to be rated high-performers. And the smallest boards were the most likely to report difficulty in finding qualified people to serve and in having more turnover than optimal. But we also found that boards with 12–20 members came from fiscally healthier organizations and were more likely than either larger or smaller boards to be using good governance practices. We expect that we're seeing the impact of both board capacity—having enough board members to fulfill fiduciary duties—and intentional design, where organizations that limit board size are also following other recommended good governance practices.

Using this information, our key recommendations to build a high-performing board follow:

PRACTICE CAREFUL BOARD MEMBER SELECTION

► The method for selecting board members matters, with external appointments and nominations hampering a board's ability to meet stewardship and fiduciary responsibilities.

► Competitive elections are linked to more positive board relations with the membership.

► Screening prospective board members for qualifications before electing them is the single most important selection method for building a high-performing board.

► Boards with diversity and representational requirements achieve minor gains in transparency, strategic performance and internal accountability.

► Terms limits also support a strong board, with the only qualification that they may give a board less time to secure feedback on its own performance.

TRAIN STAFF IN BOARD SUPPORT

► A board's performance depends on stable, professional staffing.

► ASAE membership and CAE credentialing support a CEO's role in small but beneficial ways.

► If one had to choose between hiring someone from the same field or someone trained in association management, both experiences support the CEO's role as the board's chief partner—but professional training achieves more, and tenure in the position achieves the most.

THINK STRATEGICALLY

▶ Our study finds the greater the strategic orientation, the better for board performance. But even boards that expend just a moderate amount of time on strategic thinking and planning perform better than those that do not.

▶ A lack of a strategic plan causes more problems for board performance than the choice of whether the plan is staff-led or board-led.

PRACTICE A CULTURE OF LEARNING AND ACCOUNTABILITY

▶ The choice of self-assessment tool for gauging board performance is much less important than a commitment to the process itself.

▶ Comparing boards that engage in any board development activities with the quantity of activities they employ, we find a strong case for investing in numerous training and development activities.

CHAPTER ONE

The Challenge of Good Governance: Some Background

I S THERE A RECIPE for a high-functioning board of directors? Most association leaders today—board and staff alike—would agree that effective nonprofit governance can be a challenge. Some governance experts even suggest that "effective governance by most nonprofit boards is rare and unnatural." (Taylor, Chait, and Holland, 1996: 36). Twenty-first century governance requires much more than good intentions and a passion for the mission. Boards must set an organization's strategic direction, provide active oversight to ensure that fiduciary responsibilities are accomplished, and also meet their stakeholders' expectations that resources will be used wisely (BoardSource 2010). Board members also fulfill a range of practical roles, such as providing expertise in planning and performance management, working alongside staff on programming, and participating in external relations.

Nonprofit board members are expected to perform these stewardship and oversight roles in an increasingly transparent environment, under the scrutiny of the public, the media, and regulators. Additional responsibilities are placed on association boards to meet their members' expectations. And for some organizations, these expectations have not been met. Scandal after scandal, nonprofit governance has become a "front-page story" (Chait, Ryan, and Taylor, 2005, xv).

The challenge is this: While fulfilling its legal functions may keep a board on the right side of the law, a competent board may not be a high-functioning board. Moreover, the path to high performance is not simple. Researchers have found that high-performing boards follow no obvious pattern respecting their size, makeup, or structure. The research has advanced far enough to know that boards make a difference in the effectiveness of nonprofit organizations, although not always sufficiently far to explain how they do it (Herman and Renz, 2008).

However, the prior literature tells us that strong boards share the following characteristics:

1. First, high-performing boards reflect the characteristics of "learning organizations." Learning organizations—and their boards—appreciate self-evaluation, measure progress against performance goals, and support learning and growth (see for example *7 Measures of Success*, 2006; revised edition, 2012). High-performing boards pay due attention to "process" issues such as how decisions are made, and they invest sufficiently in board development and management. They understand that whatever size, composition, and decision-making structure they choose, structure is ultimately less important than the means by which they facilitate effective decisions as a governance body.

2. High-performing boards also practice a "culture of active responsibility" (Holland and Jackson, 1998, 132–3). They take responsibility for their own performance and to how they work together. They model behaviors they expect in staff and other stakeholders,

achieving good board dynamics and cohesion. They achieve good relationships with members, chapters, and staff, and they ensure that they are themselves adequately staffed and supported.

3. Finally, high-performing boards can identify and follow effective practices. We won't call them "best practices" because context may change whether they work for every organization. But high-performing boards do use the increasingly rich literature on good governance. Readers need only look at the bibliography for this book to understand how much good advice is available to boards these days. Empirically, researchers have found that good governance practices really do matter for boards, although whether good organizations foster good boards or good boards build stronger organizations is not always clear (Herman and Renz, 1999).

Goals for this book

Given the number of publications on nonprofit governance, why one more? Nearly all research to date on nonprofit governance has been conducted on 501(c)(3) charities alone. The attention to the effectiveness of these charitable boards is important given the public-benefit nature of their work—good governance is crucial to earning the public's trust in charities.

However, all nonprofits, including the mutual benefit organizations of which associations are a part, depend on voluntary boards of directors. The problem is that the research on what these boards look like and how they perform is quite limited. This study, therefore, fills a large gap in our knowledge of the association sector, and offers association leaders a new source of high-quality, accessible data about good governance practices.

This is the first study in the United States to offer a representative snapshot of current governance practices in associations and other member-serving organizations. Our goal is evidence-driven and context-specific support for a range of effective governance practices

> ## WHAT IS A "MEMBER-SERVING ORGANIZATION"?
>
> Member-serving organizations are defined by ASAE as nonprofits that (1) hold any tax-exempt status, and (2) report some revenue in their IRS Form 990 from membership dues. While some of these organizations may call themselves "associations," we generally use the more inclusive term "member-serving organizations" in this book.
>
> When we refer to member-serving organizations in this book, we mean all of the broad group of nonprofit organizations that serve a distinct membership (see Appendix A for details). These organizations range from professional and occupational societies, to trade associations, to membership-based arts and cultural institutions, to labor unions, sports and recreational clubs, producers' cooperatives, chambers of commerce, social and fraternal clubs, and academic and learned societies. These organizations cover a broad swath of society. They can be organized under several classes of the federal tax code governing nonprofits, including as 501(c)(3), (c)(4), (c)(5), (c)(6), (c)(7), or (c)(8) organizations.

that will help association boards prepare for their responsibilities as trustees and stewards. As David Renz (2013) observes, "far too many in the [nonprofit] sector continue to base their understanding of board work on anecdote, conventional wisdom, and stories from the past." Within the association field, many observers have also called for more evidence-based practices.

Study design and rationale

Good-quality board practices—the kind that an association can bank on—tend to be industry- and field-specific. Indeed, many scholars have observed the need for more contextual, comparative, sector-specific governance research (Cornforth, 2011). This study is therefore designed to compare similar organizations and allow them to learn from one another.

Governance—defined as the legal authority held by a nonprofit board of directors—is based on group actions. Our goal is to understand how boards perform as a unit, so our survey questions asked staff to assess the board as a whole, not as individuals. And because studies also find that boards assess themselves less objectively than do observers, our survey was sent to the CEO (or executive director) of each association.

Additionally, this study is designed to present board performance as something that depends on the organization's own particular environment. In other words, boards are shaped by their internal and external environments just the same as the organizations they govern. Figure 1.1 displays this "systems" view of boards. Here, an association's ability to achieve good governance practices is dependent first organizational characteristics related to capacity, including mission, size, and external dynamics like membership growth. These shape board structure and operating norms, which in turn support board performance. This is the approach to evaluating good governance that is now recommended by nonprofit researchers because it takes into account all of the possible influences on organizational development (see, for example, Ostrower and Stone, 2010; Miller-Millesen, 2003; Cornforth, 2011). Note that we don't expect each member-serving organization to create the same approach to governance, but rather to make choices contingent on its own environment—the nature of its mission, bylaws, staffing, and so on.

Figure 1.1. A "Systems" View of Boards

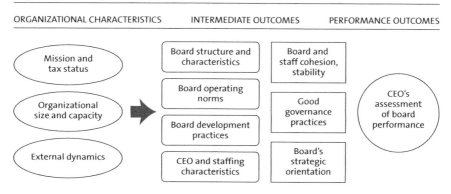

What's in this book and who should read it?

This book uses survey data on the extent to which boards of directors have achieved high performance in the eyes of executive staff. We also used the survey to identify areas of concern to the proper functioning of boards and the most promising solutions for addressing them. We produce comparable benchmark data on board structure, selection,

---

METHODOLOGY

The data come from an electronic survey of 1,585 nonprofit CEOs. All organizations with a CEO who is a member of ASAE, plus a stratified random sample of associations with no ASAE members, were invited to participate. The criteria for including the non-ASAE members in the study were that they should be U.S.-based, file their own 990 information return, have some revenue from membership dues, and have at least one paid staff member. Restricting the survey to organizations with paid staff allows us to study the relationship between board and staff members but also limits the generalizability of the results to member-serving organizations with at least one staff member.

The 15-minute survey was fielded between November 2012 and February 2013. Survey questions addressed a broad range of governance concerns, including the organizational environment; board structure; board selection procedures and challenges; the deliberative processes and the governance models they employ; board relations with staff, members, chapters, and other stakeholders; board development and self-assessment practices; and CEO assessments of board performance. Corresponding financial information drawn directly from IRS 990 forms was added later for each organization.

After one advance email, three reminder emails, one postal reminder, and after removing ineligible cases, the final response rate was 12 percent. To achieve generalizable results, the study was designed with unusual care, including human subjects review, extensive pretesting, and a weighted analysis based on several known characteristics of the population. The overall results are generalizable to similar organizations with a margin of error of 2–3 percent.

Please see Appendix A for full details on the study methodology.

---

accountability, and management practices among both organizations represented in ASAE membership and similar member-serving organizations not represented in ASAE. As mentioned earlier, results are weighted to provide the most generalizable representation possible for both ASAE members and nonmembers.

The result is relevant governance information for specific subgroups within the member-serving sector of the nonprofit world. No matter what kind of association you serve, as executive staff or as board member, this book is going to be useful to you. While we report most of our findings together, we have analyzed every survey question to determine where tax status, association field, geography, and organizational characteristics matter. So you will also find results reported out for trade associations, professional and occupational societies, for tax status, and for organizations serving mainly individuals and those serving mainly other institutions (such as trade associations). However, we only report out differences when they are significant and worthy of comment. For the most part, the reader will find more similarities than differences across organizational types.

CHAPTER TWO

A Snapshot of the Association Environment

T HIS CHAPTER PROVIDES SOME context for the challenges facing boards of directors in member-serving organizations. The respondents—CEOs and Executive Directors of these organizations—were asked to describe their field's environment in terms of level of competition, growth, the membership they serve, and other organizational characteristics. We begin with a profile of survey respondents.

Figure 2.1. CEO Training and Experience

Previously served on board or a board committee	28%
Trained or educated in the field their organization serves	52%
Trained or educated as an association professional	37%
Certified Association Executive (CAE)	21%
Another association management credential	12%

Figure 2.2. CEO Turnover

Planning to leave position in next three years	29%
Planning to leave, but undecided when	15%
Not sure	11%
Do not plan to leave position	45%

Profile of survey respondents

Among the staff—mainly self-described CEOs and executive directors—who answered this survey, 95 percent were in paid positions (note that this emphasis on paid staff was part of the study design). Before they staffed the organization, 28 percent had previously served on its board or a board committee. 52 percent described themselves as trained or educated in the field their organization serves, and 37 percent also describe themselves as trained or educated as an association professional. 21 percent hold the Certified Association Executive credential from ASAE and 12 percent hold another association management credential.

Half of our respondents had led their organizations for less than six years, and one quarter for less than three years. They brought tremendous experience to their jobs, with an average tenure in nonprofit management of 18 years of experience.

We also found the high turnover levels that have been found in other nonprofit studies. Nearly half were planning to leave their position as CEO/executive director—29 percent in the next three years and 15 percent later or undecided as to when. Eleven percent more were unsure and 45 percent more said they did not plan to leave. This information is important because prior studies have found dissatisfaction with the board to be a principal reason for CEO departures (Cornelius, et al., 2011).

Organizational characteristics

Figures 2.3 through 2.9 describe the kinds of organizations we surveyed. As Figure 2.3 displays, member-serving organizations are predominantly single organizations with no affiliates (59 percent), and to a lesser extent affiliate chapters (17 percent) or the parent organizations of affiliate chapters (24 percent). This information reflects the complex nature of nonprofit governance in the member-serving field.

Figure 2.3. Responding Organizations

Please describe the organization you are reporting about in this survey:		0% 100%
A single organization with no affiliates, chapters, or sections	59%	
An organization that serves as parent or fiscal agent for other affiliates, chapters, or sections	24%	
An affiliate, chapter, or section which files its Form 990 separately from a parent organization	17%	

Another characteristic of member-serving organizations is that they can serve both individuals and other organizations. Organizations serving mainly companies are commonly referred to as "trade associations" although they may not self-identify that way. They represent 27 percent of our sample. An additional 42 percent serve individuals and the remaining 28 percent serve a combination of individuals and organizations (Figure 2.4).

Identity-based organizations

Among those serving individuals, 11 percent of respondents came from "identity-based organizations," meaning those with a mission based on race, class, religion, veteran's status, gender, sexual orientation, or some other characteristic. We include this information because we expect these organizations to pay closer attention to board diversity.

Figure 2.4. Organizational Membership

Which best describes your organization's membership:		0% 100%
Organization serves mainly or only individuals	42%	
Organization serves mainly or only organizations or companies	27%	
Organization serves a combination of individuals and organizations	28%	

Figures 2.5, 2.6, and 2.7 display the wide diversity of organizational missions and tax statuses we find in the member-serving sector. While predominantly serving various business trades (36 percent), academic professions (6 percent) or occupations like nursing, finance, or engineering (30 percent), they also include civic and fraternal organizations (12 percent) and advocacy organizations (2 percent). In addition, a very diverse part of the charitable sector (14 percent) is engaged in direct service but with a membership base, such as historical societies, museums, youth agencies, community centers, private schools, YMCAs, and so on. This last category most represents the charitable sector at large in terms of the diversity of missions.

Among the 36 percent that self-describe as trade associations, 52 percent are in a manufacturing, mining, professional services, or sales field, 10 percent in an engineering or technical field, 8 percent in finance, 7 percent are in health or medical fields, 6 percent in education, 6 percent in agriculture, 6 percent in utilities, and 3 percent in governmental or law enforcement fields. Among the occupational societies, 33 percent are in medical professions, 17 percent in education, 16 percent in a business field, 8 percent in engineering or science, 7 percent in the public sector, 6 percent in finance, 6 percent in legal, and 3 percent in agriculture.

Tax statuses also vary, with 501(c)(3) charitable and educational organizations and 501(c)(6) business leagues predominating (Figure 2.6). All of these sub-groups fall into several tax statuses:

About three quarters of the self-described trade associations file as 501(c)(6) organizations, occupational societies split evenly between 501(c)(3) and 501(c)(6) statuses, academic societies are almost entirely 501(c)(3)s, about half the civic and fraternal clubs are 501(c)(7)s but the remainder are mainly c-3s.

Among responding organizations, 63 percent serve members who work primarily in the private sector, 19 percent serve primarily the public sector, and 15 percent serve primarily nonprofit members (Figure 2.7).

Figure 2.5. Organizational Purpose

What best describes your organization's principal purpose?		0% 100%
Academic or learned society	6%	
Occupational/professional society	30%	
Trade association	36%	
Civic, fraternal, club, or service organization	12%	
Direct service	14%	
Health research/advocacy organization	1%	
Advocacy	1%	

Figure 2.6. Tax Status

Please identify the tax status for the organization you are reporting about:		0% 100%
501(c)(3) (charitable, religious, educational, scientific)	40%	
501(c)(4) (social welfare, advocacy)	3%	
501(c)(5) (labor, agricultural)	5%	
501(c)(6) (business league)	43%	
501(c)(7) (social, recreational clubs)	6%	
Other U.S. (501(c)(8), 501(c)(9), etc.)	3%	

Figure 2.7. Membership Work Sectors

In what sector(s) do your members work?*

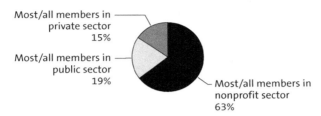

Most/all members in private sector 15%

Most/all members in public sector 19%

Most/all members in nonprofit sector 63%

* Based on the way this question was asked, total will not add up to 100%.

Chapters

Forty-five percent of the sample were single organizations with no chapter structure. Chapters (or sections) are common in the occupational society and trade association portions of the member-serving world, offering greater geographic representation and local focus for many organizations. Of the 55 percent of the sample that had chapters, the median point was 50 chapters. Overall, 20 percent had fewer than 10 chapters, an additional 25 percent had 10 to 38 chapters, 25 percent more had 39 to 116 chapters, 20 percent had 117 to 850 chapters, and the remaining 10 percent had 900 to 6000 chapters.

Geographic scope

We expect to find the geographic scope of a membership to have a lot of influence on board structure and processes. International organizations (representing 9 percent of the field) may rely more on electronic votes and possibly hold fewer board meetings. National organizations (30 percent of our sample) can also struggle with the logistics of board service, while local, state or regional organizations (61 percent) may have the advantage of limited geography.

Figure 2.8. Geographic Scope of Membership

Which most describes the geographic scope of your membership?		0% 100%
Local, state, or regional within the U.S. but not national	61%	
National: All or nearly all members are based in the U.S.	30%	
International or global: More than one quarter of members are based in other countries	9%	

External dynamics

We expect to find connections between membership trends and how CEOs rate their board's performance for two reasons. First, organizational health (as it is reflected in membership or budget growth) is likely to influence CEOs' assessments of board performance. But we also expect the external environment for these organizations to influence board member turnover and other internal dynamics. A growing organization may be more successful at attracting and keeping strong board members. An organization that operates in a competitive environment, where members must be energetically recruited, may invest more in a strong and capable board of directors.

As reflected in Figures 2.9 and 2.10, 37 percent of CEOs report an upward growth in membership over the past five years (we chose this time period to cover all of the recent recession) and 46 percent report an upward growth in budget. A smaller number of CEOs reported declines in membership (25 percent) or budget (21 percent). A similar number reported a fairly stable membership (32 percent) or budget (27percent), while 6 percent reported ups and downs or found it difficult to characterize their environment. Interestingly, only a little over half of our sample reported the same pattern of growth or decline for both their budget and membership (Figure 2.11). When asked to assess the level of competition for members between organizations serving their field or industry, nearly two thirds of our respondents reported a competitive environment (20 percent reported a high level of competition and 43 percent reported a moderate level) (Figure 2.12).

Occupational and professional societies reported healthier than average membership growth (43 percent) and budget growth (50 percent), as did academic and learned societies (37 reported membership growth and 58 percent reported budget growth). Trade associations reported below average membership growth (33 percent) and budget growth (43 percent), no doubt due to the economic downturn.

Figure 2.9. Organization's Overall Pattern of Membership Growth

How would you describe your organization's overall pattern of membership growth in the past five years?		0% 100%
Upward growth in membership	37%	
No growth/stable membership	32%	
Declining membership numbers	25%	
Ups and downs/hard to say	6%	

Figure 2.10. Organization's Overall Pattern of Budget Growth

How would you describe your organization's overall pattern of budget growth in the past five years?		0% 100%
Upward growth in budget	46%	
No growth/stable budget	27%	
Declining budget	21%	
Ups and downs/hard to say	6%	

Figure 2.11. Cross-Tabulation of Membership and Budget Growth

	Upward growth in budget	No growth/ stable budget	Declining budget	Ups and downs/hard to say	Total
Upward growth in membership	28%	5%	2%	1.6%	37%
No growth/stable membership	12%	12%	6%	1.5%	32%
Declining membership	4%	7%	12%	1.5%	25%
Ups and downs/ hard to say	2%	2%	1%	1.5%	6%
Total	46%	26%	21%	6%	100%

Figure 2.12. Level of Competition for Members Between Organizations Serving This Field or Industry

Overall, how would you assess the level of competition between organizations serving your field or industry?		0% 100%
High level of competition	20%	
Moderate amount of competition	43%	
Little competition	35%	
Don't know	1%	

Staffing

Staffing can have a lot to do with board performance and, in fact, it may be possible that staffing has a greater influence on good governance practices than any other measure of organizational capacity. For example, we expect organizations with the advantage of paid professional staff to have more time and training to support good governance than volunteer-driven organizations. We also expect turbulent staffing environments to challenge board performance, perhaps for external reasons such as board recruitment challenges, but also internal reasons such as staff capacity or because turnover signals organizational dysfunctions. Other relationships could be less predictable. For example, does an external management firm bring helpful professionalism to board support or rather limit good board-staff interactions? We'll answer that question in Chapter Six.

Among member-serving organizations in our survey population, paid professional staff predominate (84 percent), but a small number of organizations depend on an equal mix of staff and volunteers (6 percent) or mainly on volunteers (7 percent). A small number also employ external management firms (3 percent) (Figure 2.13). We also find a mix of organizational staffing sizes, with 17 percent employing 26 or more staff, 21 percent employing 11–25, and 20 percent employing 6–10 staff. The remaining 42 percent employ five or fewer staff (Figure 2.14). While staff size varied considerably across organizational types (e.g., trade associations, learned societies), how the organization was staffed did not.

With respect to staffing stability, a fortunate 56 percent of our respondents report little or no turnover among their key staff (including their own positions) in the past five years. About one third report moderate turnover, and the remaining 12 percent report high turnover affecting more than half of key positions. Staffing turnover varied little by organizational type.

When staffing structure is compared with turnover, organizations using management firms and contracts report the most stable

Figure 2.13. Organizational Staffing

		0% 100%
Staffed mainly/entirely by paid employees	84%	
Staffed mainly/entirely by volunteers	7%	
Staffed about equally by paid staff and volunteers	6%	
Staffed by a management firm or other external management contract	3%	

Figure 2.14. Number of Organizational Staff (in FTEs)

		0% 100%
0–2 staff	18%	
3–5 staff	24%	
6–10 staff	20%	
11–25 staff	21%	
26 or more staff	17%	

Figure 2.15. Turnover Rate Among Key Staff

Including the CEO, how would you describe the rate of turnover among key staff within your organization in the past five years?

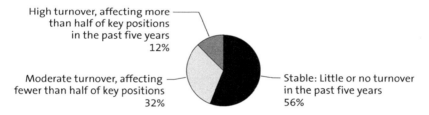

High turnover, affecting more than half of key positions in the past five years
12%

Moderate turnover, affecting fewer than half of key positions
32%

Stable: Little or no turnover in the past five years
56%

staffing and lowest turnover (Figure 2.16). One quarter to one third of those relying on their own staff report moderate turnover. Turnover decreases only a small amount as staff size increases.

Interestingly, the most volatile organizations from a staffing perspective are those that rely equally on staff and volunteers. In fact, CEO intentions to leave were not correlated with the number of staff at all, but were correlated with the type of staffing, with the unhappy CEOs nearly twice as likely to come from organizations dependent on either volunteers or a mix of volunteers and staff. This result suggests that it's harder to lead volunteer-driven organizations.

Figure 2.16. Relationship Between Rate of Staff Turnover (Horizontal) and Staffing Structure (Vertical)

	Stable, low rate of turnover	Moderate turnover	High turnover affecting more than half of key positions in past 5 yrs.	Total
Staffed mainly/entirely by paid employees (82 percent)	55%	33%	12%	100%
Staffed mainly/entirely by volunteers (6 percent)	57%	27%	16%	100%
Staffed about equally by paid staff and volunteers (6 percent)	53%	27%	20%	100%
Staffed by a management firm or external contract (3 percent)	80%	18%	2%	100%
Total	56%	32%	12%	100%

CHAPTER THREE

Board Size, Structure, and Selection

T O GAIN A FULL appreciation of what drives good governance, it is useful to begin with an understanding of a board's basic characteristics, including average size, rate of turnover, and expectations imposed on board members regarding dues and diversity. Here we also report on nominating and elections procedures, and we examine the kinds of challenges that staff report in finding qualified board members.

Board size: looking for the "sweet spot"

Well beyond the association subsector, the nonprofit sector generally has seen a great amount of discussion over the question of the best board size. Many organizations have evolved to smaller boards (sometimes called the "corporate model") in an effort to achieve greater agility and to ensure all board members are properly trained and supported in their roles. One advocate of the corporate model suggests a board size of 4–10 for publicly traded corporations (Lipman and Lipman, 2006).

KEY FINDINGS

- Association board size varies widely from 3 to 118 members, with a median of 15, and the heaviest concentration at the 12- to 15-member mark. Boards of 12–20 are more likely than either smaller or larger boards to have recommended good governance practices in place. They also represent healthier organizations with respect to membership and budget growth.

- Nearly one third of associations impose diversity or representational requirements on some board seats, but these requirements are more likely to be about membership status or geography than about gender, race, or other demographics that might improve participation by traditionally underrepresented groups.

- Three quarters of associations screen board prospects before electing them.

- In nearly three quarters of associations, board members are elected by the membership; in the remainder, boards are elected internally.

- In 15–17 percent of member-serving organizations, and even more frequently in trade associations, some board members were neither nominated nor elected by the organization they serve, but rather appointed by the board or by an affiliate.

- Despite the fact that more than half of board elections are competitive, two thirds of association CEOs report difficulty finding board members with all of the qualities they seek, most especially the ability to make the time commitment.

- Across all tax statuses, a small but troubling number of boards allow a paid CEO to preside and vote, introducing greater potential for conflicts of interest.

There's been little scholarly research on board size in non-charitable parts of the nonprofit sector. The Panel on the Nonprofit Sector and United Way membership guidelines specify a minimum of five members for charities to fulfill fiduciary duties. But governance experts also observe that there is no magic number (BoardSource, 2012b). Any decision on board size must balance more than one organizational goal, since association boards need agility as well as sufficient capacity to fulfill fiduciary duties and to meet representational goals. In a recent debate published in ASAE's *Associations Now* magazine, governance experts made strong cases for both small boards and large (Rominiecki, 2013). While small boards may have the advantage on cohesion and focus, large boards have economies of scale, can more easily populate board committees, and offer a greater diversity of perspectives.

ASAE came to a similar conclusion in *7 Measures of Success* (2006; revised edition, 2012), observing that some organizations thrive with larger boards because they have developed other processes to support efficient and effective governance. As experts note, board structure can be less important to predicting effectiveness than board process and other organizational factors (Tecker, Frankel, and Meyer, 2002). For example, Engle's (2013) research on board decision quality suggests that CEOs acquire the experience to work with larger boards over time, but that managing large boards may pose a challenge for inexperienced CEOs. From the board members' perspective, looking at BoardSource members only, Dignam (2013) found that individual board members' satisfaction with board performance varies little in boards of 13–20, but tapers off for larger boards.

The organizations in our study report a range of 3–118 voting board members, with an average of 18, a median of 15, and a standard deviation of 11. Board sizes clustered closely around the 12–15 mark, reported by 27 percent of organizations (Figure 3.1). Fewer than 1 percent of respondents reported just three or four board members;

this number is encouraging since the literature recommends (and public law and donors may require) at least five board members for effective stewardship (Panel on the Nonprofit Sector, 2007).

Trade associations preferred larger boards (average of 20 compared to the average of 16 for learned societies and 18 for professional societies). Board size was also correlated minimally but significantly (0.077, p < 0.01) with organizational age. Charities tended to prefer boards of 12–15. But contrary to BoardSource's 2010 governance study, no other organizational characteristics (geographic scope, budget size) was correlated with board size.

Figure 3.1. Number of Voting Board Members

How many voting board members did you have at the end of your last fiscal year?

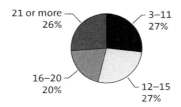

Larger boards were more likely to have an executive committee, a feature reported overall in 84 percent of these organizations. Two thirds of boards with 3–11 members reported an executive committee, compared to 94 percent of boards with 16 or more members. Executive committees are recommended by some governance experts as a means of achieving the benefits of a smaller and more nimble leadership body within a larger governance structure. However, experts also note there are risks whenever extra authority is vested in a small number of voting members, since board members share equally the fiduciary duties of nonprofit governance (Panel on the Nonprofit Sector, 2007).

Representational requirements: tax status and mission matter

Overall, 86 percent of these organizations require some or all of their board members to pay membership dues. The figure is more common in associations serving organizations than it is in associations serving individuals, but is 100 percent in 501(c)(5) labor unions, 91 percent in professional and occupational societies, and 82 percent in academic and learned societies.

We also examined diversity requirements. These can include designated board seats for members with certain demographic or other qualities, to requirements that members have certain characteristics for service on the board, to aspirations for greater diversity among board members. Diversity can cover not only race, sexual orientation, or gender, but also membership status, geography, or industry. A more diverse board has been linked to a greater strategic orientation, in part because such boards may better understand emerging membership trends (Erhardt, Werbel, and Shrader, 2003). But in practice, representational requirements can also become a barrier to high-performing boards if the board only uses diversity requirements to represent its own constituency.

The survey question read, *"Does your board have any formal goals, restrictions or requirements (imposed by bylaws, donors, or any other source) respecting the diversity or representativeness of board members? By diversity we mean any characteristic, including race, gender, etc., but also occupational status, etc."* Figure 3.2 displays the most common diversity goals and requirements reported by member-serving organizations, and compares their frequency by characteristics such as tax status.

Among member-serving organizations, 31 percent overall imposed diversity or representational requirements on board membership. Academic and learned societies (40 percent) and 501(c)(5) labor organizations (39 percent) were most likely to report they had diversity

Figure 3.2. Formal Diversity Goals, Restrictions, or Requirements for Board Members

Does your board have any formal goals, restrictions or requirements (imposed by bylaws, donors, or any other source) respecting the diversity or representativeness of board members? (Diversity means any characteristic, including race, gender, occupational status, etc.)

Note: Results are reported only for the 31 percent of associations indicating they have diversity goals.

	Total Frequency (N=495[a])	501(c)(3) (n=193)	501(c)(5) (n=32)	501(c)(6) (n=227)	Public-serving orgs. of any tax status (n=281)	Identity-based orgs. (n=75)	Trade associations (n=178)
Membership status	16.4%	13.9%	20.0%	19.8%	18.0%	21.2%	18.8%
Geographic location	14.7%	14.9%	20.0%	15.9%	15.1%	17.7%	13.8%
Gender	9.5%	11.2%	12.8%	7.6%	9.5%	23.3%	6.9%
Race/ethnicity	9.1%	11.5%	21.9%	7.1%	11.9%	19.2%	7.2%
Institution, profession, market sector	8.1%	8.5%	6.1%	9.7%	10.5%	10.1%	10.4%
Insiders, from industry or profession	7.4%	8.5%	0%	8.8%	7.3%	6.5%	9.5%
Career or experience level	6.7%	9.1%	1.0%	6.9%	6.7%	8.4%	7.7%
Age	5.8%	7.5%	7.7%	4.9%	5.3%	10.6%	4.6%
Chapter experience or affiliation	2.9%	3.3%	1.0%	3.4%	3.8%	5.2%	1.7%
Outsiders, not from industry or profession	2.7%	4.4%	0%	2.2%	2.2%	3.7%	3.1%
Professional credential	2.4%	2.2%	5.1%	2.8%	3.5%	2.0%	0.5%
Educational level	2.1%	3.1%	1.2%	1.7%	2.1%	3.7%	0.5%
Sexual orientation	2.0%	2.9%	0%	1.9%	2.0%	3.5%	0.7%
Disability	1.8%	3.4%	0%	0.8%	0.4%	5.7%	0.9%
Citizenship, lineage	0.9%	0.8%	0%	0.7%	0.6%	1.3%	0.6%

Note: Associations could be represented in more than one column.

goals and requirements, followed by trade associations (31 percent) and 501(c)(7) social and recreational clubs (21 percent). Organizations serving mainly public employees and those with identity-based missions (see Chapter Two for a definition) were also more likely to have diversity goals. This finding supports an argument we have made in other scholarship that associations serving governmental employees offer a means to achieve representational goals (Haynes and Gazley, 2011). Trade and professional associations were more likely to consider characteristics related to membership status in these diversity requirements, while membership organizations engaged in advocacy and direct service were more likely to consider biological characteristics like race and gender.

We also see from Figure 3.2 that trade associations (serving mainly business corporations) were more likely to impose representational requirements related to professions and markets, and less likely to seek representation by historically underrepresented demographic groups. Larger boards were more likely to report diversity requirements, as were organizations reporting budget growth (not shown). These relationships held true even after controlling for organizational size, age, tax status, and other characteristics. The presence of diversity goals, however, had no statistical association with organizational size or geographic scope. In fact, "international" organizations with more than one quarter of their members outside the United States were less, not more, likely to report diversity goals and requirements.

Nomination, screening, and election of board members

In place of ad hoc board member recruitment, governance experts note the value in having a standing committee with sufficient knowledge of the field to help identify and select new board members. This is often called a nominating committee. This committee can either coexist with or assume the role of a governance committee with additional board development responsibilities. Whichever structure is decided on, this committee focuses on effective recruitment and therefore supports board performance (Lakey, Hughes, and Flynn, 2004).

We found in this survey that the most common method of identifying prospective board members was indeed through a committee with nominating responsibilities (although called by different names). This was reported by 70 percent of respondents (Figure 3.3; highest in academic societies and lowest in civic clubs). In fact, one third of respondents relied only on a nominating committee, with no other means of identifying board members. In addition, 47 percent of member-serving organizations allowed board members to nominate themselves or be nominated by fellow members. The remaining methods were by executive committee (18 percent), chapters or sections (12 percent) or the CEO or other staff (12 percent).

Internal versus external nominating processes

Internal means of identifying and nominating board members represent the use of a board committee, the whole board, or staff, including the CEO. External means represent a self-nomination, membership, or chapter nomination. Overall, member-serving organizations rely on some combination of internal selection (77 percent)

Figure 3.3. Board Member Nominations

Please select all of the NOMINATIONS options currently practiced in your organization:	
By a nominating or governance committee in addition to other means* — Exclusively by a nominating or governance committee = 32%	70%
Nominate themselves or are nominated by members at large**	47%
Nominated by the executive committee*	18%
Not nominated but appointed by the board or an affiliate	15%
Nominated by chapters, sections**	12%
Nominated by the CEO*	12%

* "Internal" nominating process
** "External" nominating process

more than they do on external selection (53 percent). Occupational and professional societies, 501(c)(4) social welfare and 501(c)(5) labor organizations are more likely to rely on external means of nominating board members rather than on board committees or staff.

It's important to note that research has not tested whether one means or the other is more effective, as there are advantages and disadvantages to each. An internal nominating procedure can draw on the greater expertise by current staff and board members about desired qualities. Herman and Renz (1999) have observed, for example, that organizational effectiveness is associated loosely with a CEO's participation in board member nominations. On the other hand, an external means of nominating board members can be more democratic, transparent and effective at representing member interests.

Screening board prospects

Screening board members as part of the nominations process allows an organization to confirm a prospect's qualifications and also discuss responsibilities in advance to ensure a prospect is actively prepared to serve. Overall, 77 percent of our respondents reported formally or informally screening prospective board members to check their qualifications before an election. Charities (83 percent) and academic societies (80 percent) were considerably more likely than social welfare (55 percent) and labor organizations (45 percent), and slightly more likely than trade associations (76 percent) and social clubs (77 percent) to employ a screening process. The use of a screening process was positively correlated with having diversity goals and also with the ability to achieve those goals, but had no association with organizational or board size. Identity-based organizations were slightly more likely to employ a screening process.

Elections

When it came to voting board members into office, these member-serving organizations relied predominantly on their membership (Figure 3.4). Seventy-two percent relied on the externally oriented means of a membership vote to elect board members, compared to 24 percent for the internal process of a board vote (also known as a "self-perpetuating board"). The figure was highest for academic, professional, and trade associations (74–77 percent).

Figure 3.4. Board Member Election Process

Please select the ELECTIONS options currently practiced in your organization.	Total	501(c)(3)	501(c)(6)	Orgs with chapters
Elected by a vote of the eligible membership or a portion of the membership such as through regional elections	72%	64%	76%	74%
Elected by a vote of the board of directors	24%	36%	20%	19%
Some board members are not elected but rather appointed by the board or an affiliate	17%	17%	19%	16%
Elected by a representative group of members (such as a House of Delegates)	8%	6%	8%	15%

* Note: Respondents could select more than one option.

In 17 percent of organizations, some board members were not elected but appointed by the board or an affiliated organization. An additional 8 percent used an indirect method of membership election via a house of delegates (highest in academic societies).

In some associations (namely, 501(c)(6) professional and trade associations, those with a chapter structure and those serving mainly individuals), boards relied more heavily on their membership or a house of delegates to elect new members. By contrast, 501(c)(3) charities were much more likely to rely on an internal means of electing board members, with more than one third employing a board vote. The difference between charities and other members-serving organizations most likely rests on the fact that the bylaws for many charities may include a membership structure but may still entrust less electoral responsibility in the membership compared to the mutual-benefit organizations that predominate outside the 501(c)(3) tax status.

Competitive elections

Shown in Figure 3.5, a slight majority of member-serving organizations report elections are competitive sometimes (37 percent) or always (17 percent). Academic (42 percent) and professional societies (28 percent) are most likely to report elections are always competitive. Trade associations (51 percent) and direct service membership organizations (76 percent) are most likely overall to report elections are never competitive. Boards that relied on internal nominations (such as a slate of board members forwarded by a nominating committee) were less likely to have competitive elections, while organizations with chapter structures were more likely to rely on open nominations and to hold competitive elections.

Figure 3.5. Board Election Competitiveness

How often are your board member elections competitive, with more than one individual running for the same seat?

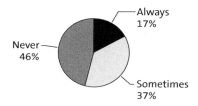

Challenges in finding qualified board members

Which selections processes make it easiest to find board members? Overall, 65 percent of CEOs reported that it was somewhat or very difficult to find qualified board members (Figure 3.6). The qualities most sought by association CEOs were strategic thinking and leadership skills, fundraising or giving abilities, an interest in the

Figure 3.6. Difficulty in Finding Qualified People to Serve as Board Member

How difficult would you say it is to find qualified people to serve on your organization's board?

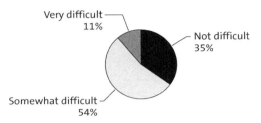

Very difficult 11%

Not difficult 35%

Somewhat difficult 54%

organization's mission, professional qualifications (especially in associations representing a small field), and representation from racial and ethnic minorities. More than 100 respondents each mentioned prior board experience, marketing and communications, and finance or management skills as difficult to find (Figure 3.7).

Figure 3.7. Qualifications Sought by Respondents Reporting Difficulty in Finding Qualified Board Members

If you responded that it is "somewhat" or "very" difficult to find qualified individuals to serve on your board, what kind of challenges do you face?		0%　　　　　　　　　100%
Board members who can make the time commitment	45%	
Board members with required breadth of knowledge or experience	27%	
Board members who can manage expense, travel, or other logistics of board service	14%	
Board members with specific required qualifications	14%	

These results varied little by organizational type (results not shown), with academic societies and trade associations having a slight advantage with respect to the ease of finding board members. Relying on chapters and sections to identify board members appeared to lessen the difficulty in finding board members, but variations in the use of other internal or external nominations processes had little effect on a CEO's concern about the ability to find board members.

Direct appointments: proceed with caution

As reflected in Figures 3.3 and 3.4, in 15–17 percent of member-serving organizations, some board members were neither nominated nor elected by the organization they serve, but rather appointed by the board or by an affiliate. This practice happens slightly more frequently in larger trade associations. Coalition-type organizations can use direct appointments to meet important representational goals, and these members may still have been elected democratically by some other organization. However, an alternative method of selecting some members onto a board can reduce a board's sense of cohesion. Such a practice can also introduce conflicts of interest.

When we compared the organizations employing some direct appointments against those using other board selection methods, we found that organizations using this practice experienced lower CEO assessments of board performance (results not shown). The boards with direct appointments were slightly more likely to experience the removal of a board member before a term was up (58.7 percent vs. 55.8 percent). CEOs cited a board member's inability to fulfill a board duty more frequently as a reason for removal (4.1 percent vs. 2.4 percent), although not necessarily because of a conflict of interest (all reported results are statistically significant, employing Levene's test for equality of variances).

The CEOs of these organizations were slightly more likely to report poor relationships among board members, and between board and staff (all reported results statistically significant). They were also nearly twice as likely to report poor board relations with chapters (12.2 percent versus 7.5 percent). They rated their boards lower overall on accountability to members, direct engagement with members, willingness to secure feedback, and willingness to take responsibility for decisions. Of particular concern was a lower rating on the board's ability to make independent decisions that are not based on self-interest (with 18.6 percent of boards with direct appointments rated as "needing improvement" compared to 13.4 percent elsewhere), and also a lower rating on the board's ability to lead in a way that maintains the public trust (9.5 percent rated as "needs improvement" vs. 5.1 percent elsewhere).

These results suggest that for many boards, direct appointments are less effective than open nominations and elections processes in building a cohesive and collegial board atmosphere, and forging strong board-staff, board-member, and board-chapter relations. They paint the picture of a board that is less in touch with stakeholder groups. While many other measures of board performance were not related to this board selection strategy, direct appointments could be risky to board performance unless this practice is balanced with more effective nominating processes and accompanied by good governance strategies to control the potential harm.

CEO's role on the board: avoiding conflicts of interest?

Reported by 57 percent of associations, the most common role for the CEO is as an ex-officio and non-voting member of the board. This role is most consistent with good governance practices (BoardSource 2012a). However 14 percent of CEOs overall report they are a voting member of the board (Figure 3.8). More alarming, 6 percent of our respondents (n=96) are both paid staff members and the presiding, voting member of the board. BoardSource found a similar figure in its 2012 study of BoardSource members (mainly charities).

This problem appears across all tax statuses and organizational types, although in differing amounts. In 501(c)(5) labor organizations, 44 percent of CEOs have a vote on the board, while in 501(c)(6) business leagues, 9 percent of CEOs have a vote. In 501(c)(3) charities, 14 percent allow the CEO to vote and 12 percent allow the CEO to

Figure 3.8. CEO's Role on the Board

According to your bylaws, what best describes (your) the CEO's role on the board of directors?		0%	100%
The CEO is an ex-officio, non-voting member of the organization's board	57%		
The CEO is a voting member of the organization's board	14%		
The CEO is not a member of the organization's board	25%		
The bylaws specify another role	4%		

preside. Governance experts would be concerned about people who serve in both a key staff position and as a voting member of the board, since this role makes it more difficult for them to avoid conflicts of interest and to exercise independent judgment about the organization's strategy and finances. Even in for-profit corporations, where the practice is more widespread, there seems to be some connection between the practice of allowing CEOs to serve as board chair and the board's difficulty in performing fiduciary duties as effectively.

Length of board service: most organizations follow recommended practices

Term lengths describe the number of years a board member can serve before a reelection is required. Ideally, these details are included in organizational bylaws. They are a recommended practice, under the expectation that "the board should establish clear policies and procedures addressing the length of terms and number of consecutive terms a board member may serve" (Panel on the Nonprofit Sector, 2007).

In this study, 89 percent of member-serving organizations overall reported having specific term lengths, with variation ranging from 93–94 percent in academic, professional and social clubs and societies, to 87 percent in trade associations (Figure 3.9). Recent research by BoardSource (2010) found that 71 percent of charitable organizations

Figure 3.9. Percentage of Organizations That Have Policies Specifying Board Member Term Lengths

Does your organization have a policy specifying the number of years of a board term?

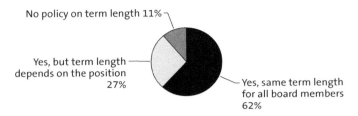

No policy on term length 11%

Yes, but term length depends on the position 27%

Yes, same term length for all board members 62%

had term lengths; we found term lengths in 89 percent of charities with members. The difference may rest in the greater reliance that member-serving organizations place on active representation of members through the board, something easier to achieve with regular board turnover. Among member-serving organizations, 61 percent report a three-year term (compared to 71 percent found by BoardSource's 2010 study). An additional 25 percent report a two-year length, 5 percent report one-year terms, and 9 percent report terms of four to six years. About one in three reported that the term length depended on the board position (results not shown).

Respecting term limits, or number of times a board member can renew a term before leaving the board, 9 percent of associations have no policy on term limits, 11 percent allow one term only, 39 percent allow two terms, and 14 percent allow three or more terms (Figure 3.10). An additional 27 percent either have no term limits or allow board members to sit out a period of time and return to the board.

The 37 percent of associations with either no policy or no term limits is consistent with an estimate reported in past BoardSource (2012b) research, where two out of five charitable boards had no term limits. As a comparison, the number of boards with term limits in the corporate sector is much lower. However, in the nonprofit sector,

Figure 3.10. Board Member Term Limits

How many terms altogether can a board member serve in a regular non-officer's position?		0% 100%
No policy	9%	
One term	11%	
Two terms	39%	
Three or more terms	14%	
No limit, or board members can sit out a period of time and return to the board	27%	

many governance experts would consider term limits a preferred practice, since such limits allow organizations to rotate members, bring in new ideas and perspectives, and reduce board member burnout (BoardSource, 2012a). In fact, term limits may improve board performance overall (Bradshaw, Murray, and Wolpin, 1992). We will test this proposition further in Chapter Six.

Board member turnover: achieving the right balance

Turnover on boards describes the frequency with which board members leave their positions. Turnover in boards that already have term limits can obviously be orchestrated, as a means of bringing in new expertise and fresh perspectives. For example, board turnover can help an association maintain active representation as member demographics change. But board members can also decide to leave their positions before a term has expired. Whether their departure is out of dissatisfaction or for more benign reasons (a job change, a move) it can create challenges for boards to fill the vacancy.

We examined both the rate of turnover overall and the frequency with which board members left their positions before their terms were up (Figure 3.11). When asked, 77 percent of CEOs reported they had the right level of board turnover to achieve a balance between institutional knowledge and new perspectives, while 17 percent described

Figure 3.11. Turnover Rate Among Board Members

How would you assess the rate of turnover among your organization's board members?		0%　　　　　100%
We have more turnover than optimal / I'd like to see board members stay longer than they do.	6%	
We have about the right amount of board member turnover to achieve a balance between institutional knowledge and new perspectives.	77%	
We have less turnover than optimal.	17%	

less turnover than optimal and 6 percent described more turnover than optimal.

Although nearly one quarter of respondents reported more than optimal or less than optimal board turnover, we looked for a relationship between board and staff turnover (Figure 3.12). The problem does not appear to be widespread, since nearly half (46 percent) of CEOs reported both the right amount of staff turnover and the right amount of board turnover in their organizations, and two thirds reported the right amount of board turnover and only minimal to moderate staff turnover. Younger organizations were more likely to

Figure 3.12. Comparing Rates of Staff and Board Turnover

	More board turnover than optimal	About the right amount of board member turnover	Less turnover than optimal	Total
Stable: little or no staff turnover in the past five years	2%	46%	8%	56%
Moderate staff turnover, affecting fewer than half of key positions	2%	22%	7%	32%
High staff turnover, affecting more than half of the key positions in past five years	2%	9%	2%	12%
Total	6%	77%	17%	100.0%

report both high staff and high board turnover, although they were also more likely to report upward growth in membership and budget.

Since member-serving organizations must also balance board member turnover against their ability to retain enough board members who have the institutional knowledge and expertise they need for effective governance, we also compared policies on terms to rates of board member turnover. The results displayed in Figure 3.13 suggest that CEOs in associations with no term limits, as well as those allowing three or more terms, are much more likely to report a lower than optimal rate of board member turnover. Some nonprofit staff and board members alike may express general concern about their ability to retain board members, but term limits don't appear to be the culprit and seem to play an important role in ensuring healthy board turnover.

Figure 3.13. Comparing CEO Assessments of Board Turnover Rate Against Association Policy on Term Limits

	No policy	One term	Two terms	Three or more terms	No limit, or members can return after sitting out a time period
More turnover than optimal	14%	2%	5%	5%	8%
About the right amount of turnover	73%	93%	84%	79%	67%
Less turnover than optimal	13%	5%	11%	16%	25%
	100%	100%	100%	100%	100%

Where and when does board size matter?

Does board size relate to other structural characteristics of the board in a way that helps associations understand the optimal board size? BoardSource (2010, p. 18) has argued that "the very structure of board service—size, terms, and officers—shapes board culture and practices in a variety of ways." Although not in a representative study, BoardSource found a "sweet spot" in boards of 15–22 members with respect to CEO performance ratings and good governance practices.

We compared our two rough quartiles: boards of 12–15 and those with 16–20 members. We conclude that there is no clear advantage between these two groups, but both have advantages over larger and smaller boards. For example, boards of 12–15 members were more likely than either smaller or larger boards to have policies in place for term lengths, to limit the number of terms a board member could serve, to use tracking methods for reporting diversity goals, and to report competitive elections (results not shown; note that these

• • • • • • • •

There is no clear advantage between boards of 12–15 members compared to boards with 16–20, but both have advantages over larger and smaller boards.

• • • • • • • •

are correlations only). Compared to boards either larger or smaller, those with 12–15 members seemed to represent healthier organizations, where CEOs reported upward budget and membership growth, and less competition for members. CEOs with boards of 12–15 were considerably more likely to report having the right amount of board member turnover, even though they were also more likely to report that their organization held competitive elections for board members. They were least likely to report having difficulty finding qualified board members. These organizations also had CEOs who were less likely to be considering leaving their job.

Boards of 16–20 members were most likely to perform board development activities, and also less likely to report high staff turnover. They were more likely to have diversity requirements or representational goals, and also more likely than either larger or smaller boards to engage in high levels of strategic discussion at board meetings.

Both the boards with 12–15 members and 16–20 members were much more likely to perform screening of nominees. They were also half as likely to have the CEO serving as presiding officer than either smaller or larger boards.

Comparing the largest and smallest boards, the smallest boards—rather than the largest—were the most likely to report difficulty in finding qualified people to serve and in having more turnover than optimal. Largest boards were least likely to evaluate their own performance.

· · · · · · · · · · · ·

The smallest boards—rather than the largest—were the most likely to report difficulty in finding qualified people to serve and in having more turnover than optimal.

· · · · · · · · · · · ·

CHAPTER FOUR

Board Operating Norms and Decision Making

A KEY QUESTION ABOUT BOARD operating norms and procedures is how boards best structure themselves to meet their fiduciary duties and to focus on strategic rather than operational matters. In this chapter, we report on the range of ways in which association boards of directors operate, including how often boards meet together and how the board spends its meeting time.

Number and nature of board meetings

Regular meetings are considered a necessary governance practice, since they not only allow board members to exercise the duty of care but also offer the benefits of personal interaction and a healthy exchange of ideas (Panel on the Nonprofit Sector, 2007). There is no prescribed minimum number of board meetings in the way there is a prescribed range of board members. At least some charity governance authorities suggest that with a strong committee structure and

KEY FINDINGS

- Association boards have no strong preference for number of meetings per year, but the mean number is six.

- CEOs value the deliberative board processes that can support consensus-based decision-making.

- Nearly two thirds of boards always or nearly always vote unanimously.

- Board chairs play a much more central role in getting board work done than do other board officers.

- The most common use of board time is receiving reports from staff, but more half of member-serving boards spend at least 25 percent of their meeting time on strategic thinking and discussion.

depending on mission, even one meeting per year may be sufficient (Panel on the Nonprofit Sector, 2007).

In this study, member-serving organizations displayed no consistency in meeting preferences, with one third of the full board meeting face-to-face just one to three times per year, an additional one third meeting four to six times per year, and the remainder meeting seven or more times per year. The mean number of meeting times was six, and the median number was four. Figure 4.1 displays the frequency of board meetings in more detail. As expected, the geographic scope of the membership plays a large role in meeting frequency, with national and international organizations meeting less than half as often (average of three meetings) as local, regional and state organizations (average of eight).

Tax status and field also were factors in determining meeting frequencies, with the boards of 501(c)(5) labor organizations and 501(c)(7) social clubs meeting most frequently (average of 9–10 times

Figure 4.1. Frequency of Board Meetings

	Overall Frequency (1585)	Local/ Regional/ state (n=965)	National (n=476)	International (n=144)
No face-to-face meetings, electronic only	0.6%	0.5%	0.6%	0.7%
1–2 per year	17%	5%	35%	40%
3–4 per year	36%	26%	53%	47%
5–6 per year	15%	20%	7%	6%
7–9 per year	5%	8%	0.8%	0.6%
10–11 per year	11%	17%	1%	2%
12 per year	11%	16%	0.9%	4%
More than 12 per year	4%	6%	1%	0.0%

per year). 501(c)(3) member-serving organizations met an average of eight times per year. Academic and learned societies met together just 3.5 times a year on average, occupational and professional societies met an average of five times per year, and trade associations met an average of six times a year.

Fifty-four percent of member-serving organizations reported the board also met electronically in addition to face-to-face meetings, with an average of two additional conference calls or other long-distance means of communicating. When electronic meetings are combined with face-to-face meetings, the median increases to seven annual interactions between board members.

How are decisions made?

Formal processes
Boards commonly define their decision-making processes through formal rules. Using bylaws or another formal policy to define how decisions will be made can also be considered a recommended practice, since it creates a transparent, fair, and consistent means of establishing this key board function (Tesdahl, 2010). More than

99 percent of the boards in this study relied on formal processes such as motions and votes for decision-making, and 68 percent of association executives described them as very important.

When it came to the specific options for making decisions, *Robert's Rules of Order* was described as "very important" by only 23 percent of respondents and as "fairly important" by 29 percent more, with the remainder assigning this parliamentary system of deliberation little or no value in their decision-making. In addition to *Robert's Rules,* a few association CEOs mentioned Glenn Tecker's Knowledge Based Decision-making Process, the Carver Policy Governance model, the Dialogue before Deliberation approach, and the American Institute of Parliamentarians Standard Code of Parliamentary Procedure as tools they employed. Interestingly, neither the size of the organization nor its geographic scope was associated with a greater reliance on formal decision-making tools. But boards of 12–15 in size were more likely than either their smaller or larger counterparts to rely on formal processes.

Informal processes

Respondents were divided on the value of informal board discussion as a decision-making tool, with one quarter finding little or no value in the strategy and the remainder more likely to rate the strategy as fairly rather than very important. One executive was employed by an association where "sunshine rules" prevented board members from discussing association business anywhere except for the boardroom. Many described "thumbs up, down, or sideways" votes and other informal straw poll methods to reach consensus before formal votes. For example, one CEO described a preference for Sturgis' parliamentary procedures as an alternative to *Robert's Rules of Order* when leading informal discussion at board meetings because they freed the board to act on more than formal motions. International associations (those with more than one-quarter of their members outside of the U.S.) and organizations with larger boards were much more likely to assign value to informal board discussion as a means of making decisions, and this result makes sense when one considers the greater difficulty these organizations might have in convening the full board in one place.

Deliberative processes

Some processes, whether formally or informally adopted, emphasize open discussion and deliberation before a vote is taken. Many can facilitate consensus-based decisions, which were considered important by nearly three quarters of all respondents (39 percent ranked them fairly important and 48 percent ranked them very important). For example, one CEO observed, "The only time we follow Robert's Rules closely is during our house of delegates [because] Roberts can interfere with consensus-based discussions." Several others mentioned that even when Robert's Rules were used, it was important to hold a full board discussion of a motion before voting.

One of the more interesting findings is that the larger and more international associations were slightly more likely to value consensus-based decision making, and less likely to rely on formal parliamentary tools such as *Robert's Rules of Order* or its variations. This finding suggests that meeting the greater challenges associated with size and geography does not necessarily require a parliamentary process. Again, the "sweet spot" for this practice was within boards of 12–15 in size. The larger organizations were also more likely to use a planned board retreat as a meeting tool, another forum that emphasizes discussion and group process.

The greater goal of a deliberative process is the ability to make informed decisions. A common deliberative process in governance is to rely on committees or task forces to fully air issues before bringing them to a full board for a decision. Many respondents discussed the value of committee reports, or policy issue analysis papers, white papers created by staff or board members, and other means by which information could be exchanged before a vote. They also observed that these written reports required other board members to prepare for meetings in advance. One executive director observed that "board members' preparation in advance of the meeting is critical to healthy discussion and decision making."

"Consent agendas" were also mentioned as strategies that allow boards to limit procedural votes and spend more time on discussion about larger issues. Consent agendas package routine and non-controversial items such as meeting minutes into a single vote with limited discussion. Board members are expected to review these items in advance. Although considered an effective practice in much of the governance literature, there was no consensus in our study on their value, with 35 percent of respondents describing consent agendas as very important, 25 percent as fairly important, while a further 39 percent gave them little or no importance. Boards of 12–15 in size, along with academic and professional societies, were the most likely to use consent agendas.

> • • • • • • • • • • •
> *"A strong board chair and CEO makes a big difference in how time and the agenda are managed at the meetings. The critical thing is the partnership/relationship between the board chair and CEO."*
> – a survey respondent
> • • • • • • • • • •

Several dozen respondents mentioned the value of allowing email voting between board meetings to attend to simple decisions that did not require discussion.

Effective meeting practices

An annual general meeting was considered very important by one third of all respondents, with 15 percent not holding one at all. International associations were most likely to value an annual meeting, but larger associations by staff size were less likely to value the effectiveness of the annual meeting.

Teleconferencing

Overall, 45 percent of sampled associations did not allow board members to attend meetings electronically (such as by conference call, depending on what state laws allow). Some legislators and nonprofit organizations consider teleconferencing to be a breach of the fiduciary duty of care. However, for a national or international organization, geography makes frequent in-person meetings difficult, so the growth of affordable telecommunications options is a real benefit.

Of those organizations allowing electronic meeting attendance, respondents were divided equally on whether the practice had none or some value to the board. For understandable reasons, local, state and regional associations placed the least value on teleconferencing as a meeting tool, while two thirds of national and international associations considered the practice to be fairly or very effective. In comments, many respondents discussed the challenges they faced in making electronic communication work as a governance tool. CEOs observed the value of face-to-face meetings and the need to strike a balance. According to one respondent, "Prior to 2010, all board meetings were face-to-face and held in different locations around the state. Since then, most meetings are online. When it has been possible to have [an extra] face-to-face meeting, the benefits for discussion and relationship building have been noticeable to all." Respondents were more likely to note the value of using email, email lists, and other electronic tools to share information among board members, rather than only via meetings.

Voting

In most of these organizations, board votes appear to be always or nearly always unanimous (Figure 4.2). This is not necessarily a bad thing: Unanimous votes can signal that board members have reached consensus on decisions. And high-functioning boards can also speak with one voice even when they do not pass unanimous votes (Carver, 1997). But if boards are always voting unanimously, a red flag can be raised about how actively they are engaged in governance. Unanimous voting can reflect a passive board that relies on rubber-stamping staff decisions. We will return to the question of what impact this practice has on board performance in Chapter Six.

Figure 4.2. Frequency of Unanimous Board Votes

How often does the board vote unanimously on a decision?	
Always or nearly always	64%
Often	34%
Usually not	2%
Total	100%

Who gets the work done?

Respondents were asked, "Aside from staff, when you consider all of the work accomplished by your board of directors, please describe how important each of the following individuals or groups are to getting the work done." Responses, displayed in Figure 4.3, suggest that board responsibility rests heavily on the chair and other officers. Although many organizations have found informal task forces and ad hoc committees to offer a way of delegating board work to a wider group of willing volunteers, we found that these ad hoc methods were not considered important by many of our respondents.

We received many additional comments about this question. More than one CEO expressed dissatisfaction with board member

Figure 4.3. Board Task Assignments

Who gets the work done?	We don't use this	Of little importance	Fairly important	Very important	Total
The presiding board officer (e.g., chair)	2%	7%	30%	61%	100%
Board officers and/or executive committee	2%	13%	42%	43%	100%
Other formal, standing committees	5%	19%	47%	30%	100%
Informal task forces and ad hoc committees	9%	27%	46%	19%	100%

engagement. One wrote, "As a caveat, all are important to getting the work done, but in reality we struggle unless certain individuals are on the committee. Then, those individuals are all over-worked." Another commented, "I wish the board did take lead roles in getting the work done. It is a matter that is being addressed … and it will no longer be a rubber stamp process but a roll up your sleeves, hands-on working board." More than one told us that this question made no sense unless we listed "staff" first. One individual observed that in their case, only one committee had made the difference, but for the better: "The Governance committee has to be pulled out separately in our case. It saw the need for changes and brought term limits, fresh blood, accountability, and an outside consultant to totally change the governance culture."

How does the board use its meeting time?

When listed in order of frequency, boards of member-serving organizations are most likely to be receiving and discussing reports and information from staff and committees. Two thirds of boards are spending more than one quarter of their meeting time on this activity. The rest of their time is spent in financial oversight (less than one quarter of meeting time for about 61 percent of boards), policy review (less than one quarter of total meeting time for about 70 percent of

Figure 4.4. Time Usage During Board Meetings

How does the board use meeting time?	None	Less than 25% of meeting time	25–50% of meeting time	More than 50% of meeting time	Total
Receiving/discussing reports and information from staff and committees	1%	32%	48%	19%	100%
Strategic thinking and discussion	2%	45%	40%	13%	100%
Reviewing/discussing financial statements or the budget	0.5%	61%	31%	7%	100%
Reviewing/discussing/setting policies and procedures	4%	66%	26%	5%	100%
Monitoring programs and services	8%	57%	31%	4%	100%
Monitoring/evaluating the CEO and other staff who report directly to the board	19%	72%	8%	1%	100%
Discussing the board's own goals and performance	29%	59%	11%	1%	100%

boards), and program oversight (less than one quarter of meeting time for about two thirds of boards).

More problematic is the finding that one in five boards (19.2 percent) do not spend any time monitoring and evaluating the CEO and staff who report directly to the board. Some boards will delegate this task to a committee, but even so, governance experts recommend that the full board participate at some point in discussion and action (Panel on the Nonprofit Sector, 2007). Boards also spend very little time discussing their own goals and performance; 29 percent do none of this at all.

Achieving a strategic focus in board meetings

Governance experts recommend board meetings that are focused on strategic rather than operational issues. This is, for example, a core element of Carver's Policy Governance Model. The Panel on the

Nonprofit Sector outlines the responsibility for charitable boards thus: "the board should establish and review regularly the organization's mission and goals." Therefore, it is encouraging to find that over half of member-serving boards spend at least 25 percent of their meeting time on strategic thinking and discussion.

We asked a related question about the board's level of strategic activity. When asked how strategic planning is carried out in their organization, two thirds (68 percent) of association CEOs reported that the staff and board work jointly to develop the strategic plan, and an additional 7.2 percent reported that the board accomplished this role on its own. However, one-quarter reported that they either did not have a strategic plan (with little variation among organizational types) or that staff developed the plan without board participation. Even if these plans might later be approved by the board or membership, these organizations have a less than optimal level of board engagement in strategic planning.

Figure 4.5. Level of Organizational Strategic Activity

What process best describes how strategic planning is carried out in your organization? Please choose the single best answer.	
At present, we do not have a strategic plan	13%
Staff develops the plan, which the board and/or membership approves	12%
Staff and board work jointly to develop strategic plan	68%
Board develops and approves strategic plan on its own	7%
Total	100%

CHAPTER FIVE

"Good Governance" Practices in Member-Serving Organizations

W HAT ARE THE BOARDS of member-serving organizations doing to meet public and member expectations? Governance experts have become strong proponents of more active boards, arguing that boards must also engage in their own training and education, and assess their own performance. Among charitable 501(c)(3) organizations, if not more broadly across the nonprofit sector, the public also expects a certain level of transparency (in fact, Charity Navigator recently added this quality to its ranking system).

These broader expectations for charities are reflected in BoardSource publications, such as the "12 Principles of Good Governance" and in the Panel on the Nonprofit Sector's "Principles for Good Governance and Ethical Practice" (see sidebars on following pages).

The Association Forum of Chicagoland (2011, 2012) has taken a leading role in developing standards of practice for member-serving associations of any tax status. These standards include the expectation

KEY FINDINGS

- Member-serving organizations that formally tracked board representational goals were more likely to report that they meet the goals.

- In the past two years, two thirds of boards experienced at least one of the following circumstances: failure to produce a quorum at a regularly scheduled meeting, failure of a board member to complete a term of office, or policy conflicts between the board and staff or between members and the board that required board action.

- Organizations represented in ASAE membership were considerably more likely than non-ASAE members to use board development tools.

- While four out of five associations practiced at least one form of board training, only half of boards assessed their own performance or set performance goals for themselves. Only 3 percent assessed their performance in relationship to a strategic or business plan.

- Staff time spent on board support had little to do with organizational size and pays off in fewer board problems and more board development.

that governance appointments should be both skills based and talent based, and that they should be shielded from parochial and individual interests. Governing units should have clearly defined outcomes and should hold themselves accountable for their work. The size of a governance structure should be kept to the minimum necessary to produce results. Additional expectations of association board members are also included in the sidebar on page 68.

12 PRINCIPLES OF GOOD GOVERNANCE

A leading source of good governance expertise, BoardSource (2005), describes 12 desirable board competencies. High performing boards:

1. Have a constructive partnership with staff
2. Are mission driven
3. Engage in strategic thinking
4. Promote a culture of inquiry
5. Practice independent mindedness
6. Promote an ethos of transparency
7. Comply with laws with high integrity
8. Can steward and sustain resources
9. Are results oriented
10. Engage in intentional board practices
11. Engage in continuous learning
12. Energize and revitalize themselves

Achieving transparency

Transparency on a nonprofit board can be achieved by the openness with which a board reports on organizational-level or board-level goals and accomplishments to the membership or public. Since we looked at whether member-serving nonprofits had representational requirements, we also asked CEOs to tell us if they reported their progress in meeting these board-level representational requirements to stakeholders (Figure 5.1). Most reported they did, although they were more likely to report progress internally, such as to a nominating committee, than externally to members, donors, or regulators. Labor organizations were most likely to report their progress on these goals to their membership (14 percent), but 501(c)(3) and 501(c)(4) organizations were most likely to report multiple methods of tracking and reporting goals. Unfortunately, about one in four (23 percent) of organizations that have formal rules on representation do not track their progress.

As Figure 5.2 reflects, boards are usually able to meet these representational goals. Fifty-nine percent meet them all of the time, and

Figure 5.1. Method for Documenting, Tracking, or Reporting Representational Goals and Requirements*

Internally	62%
To the membership	28%
In the annual report	12%
On the webpage	11%
To contractors, donors, or regulators	5%
Do not track	23%

* Includes only those indicating their board has formal goals, restrictions, or requirements respecting the diversity or representativeness of board members.

Figure 5.2. Organizational Achievement of Representational Goals and Requirements

In the past three years, how successful has your organization been at achieving these diversity goals?

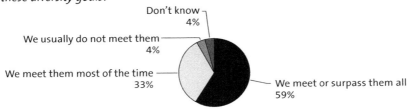

Don't know — 4%

We usually do not meet them — 4%

We meet them most of the time — 33%

We meet or surpass them all — 59%

33 percent meet them most of the time. Member-serving organizations that formally track board representational goals were more likely to report that they meet the goals. The greatest success at meeting representational goals happens in organizations that report progress to their membership or the public, as opposed to those that report only internally or to donors and contractors. This result suggests that tracking and publicly reporting representational goals for board membership may help discipline organizations to achieve the goals.

• • • • • •

Publicly reporting representational goals for board membership may help discipline organizations to achieve the goals.

• • • • • •

Fulfilling the duty of care

The most basic way that board members reflect their fiduciary "duty of care" in their work is by showing up. In the past two years, CEOs in our study reported that 17 percent of boards failed to produce a quorum at a regularly scheduled meeting. In addition, 57 percent of CEOs reported that a board member failed to complete a term of office either through resignation or by action of the board. The most common reasons given were personal reasons (26 percent) or a change in employment or some other qualification that made them ineligible

"PRINCIPLES FOR GOOD GOVERNANCE AND ETHICAL PRACTICE"

Completed in 2007 under the leadership of Independent Sector, the "Principles" are a public document intended to encourage stronger self-regulation within the charitable sector. Many of the 33 principles address governance expectations, including the following:

- Boards should have policies and procedures in place to manage conflicts of interest.
- Boards should have policies and procedures to protect whistleblowers.
- Information about how the organization is governed and managed should be widely available to the public.
- The board should review and approve strategy, policy and finances.
- The board should meet regularly enough to fulfill its duties, and should have an attendance policy.
- Organizations with paid staff should separate the roles of CEO, Board Chair and Treasurer.
- Boards should communicate internally to ensure all board members understand their fiduciary duties.
- Boards should evaluate their performance at least every three years.
- Board terms and lengths of service should be clearly identified.
- Boards should monitor financial activities.

to complete their term (18 percent overall—but 35 percent in trade associations). But 19 percent also reported board members who were unable to fulfill attendance obligations, and 3.5 percent reported the removal was due to a conflict of interest.

Additionally, nine percent of CEOs reported policy conflicts between the board and staff that required board action, and 11 percent reported conflicts between members and the board. Overall, two thirds of boards experienced at least one of the circumstances described above.

Ensuring board members are prepared for the job

While there is more scrutiny of board performance in the present day, there is also considerably more professional training available to help board members succeed in their roles. Board training can include a formal orientation, job descriptions, consultants and trainers, mentoring, retreats, and other forms of board development. Board development can also include training for chief staff in supporting board members effectively.

Figure 5.3 displays the frequency of board training and educational activities for member-serving organizations. Overall, 82 percent used at least one method and just 18 percent of respondents reported they used none of the methods listed below. The majority of boards rely on a formal orientation and/or a board manual. One third of the full sample relied on just one or two methods of board training.

• • • • • • • • •

Occupational societies and organizations represented in ASAE membership were considerably more likely than others to use board development tools.

• • • • • • • • •

continued on page 70

FIDUCIARY AND MANAGEMENT DUTIES FOR THE ASSOCIATION EXECUTIVE AND GOVERNING BODY

1. Place the association's interests above their own, and refrain from using their position of trust to further their own personal gain.

2. Provide association executives with a collaborative working relationship and an atmosphere conducive to the fulfillment of both the executive's and the governing body's respective duties as fiduciaries.

3. Recognize that the chief executive officer is the agent for the organization and allow the CEO to operate in that context.

4. Exercise due diligence in performance of their governance role.

5. Refrain from disclosing any confidential association information acquired in the performance of their duties, except as permitted by the association or required by law.

6. Recognize that the governing body serves as entrusted by the membership and consequently is responsible for the integrity of governance and for its own development, discipline, and performance.

7. Provide accountability to the membership or other constituents when applicable through regular reporting.

8. Review financial statements and operating reports conscientiously, ensuring that the organization is performing in accordance with its mission, strategic plan, and/or operating plan.

9. Recognize that budget review is an important authorization process, by reviewing proposed budgets conscientiously and asking appropriate questions about the budget.

10. Provide for and review an annual audit by an independent auditor who reports directly to the board, giving prompt and decisive attention to any recommendations including "material weaknesses" and "significant deficiencies" it may contain.

11. Establish a procedure for the annual review of the IRS form 990.

12. Establish and monitor policies and procedures to safeguard the assets and future viability of the organization.

continued on next page

continued from previous page

13. Provide for a risk prevention program, which includes but is not limited to obtaining the appropriate directors' and officers' liability and other insurance coverage.

14. Exercise the governing body's duties in good faith and in a manner that is in the best interest of the organization.

15. Perform their duties in accordance with applicable statutes and the terms of the organization's bylaws and other governing documents; act within the powers conferred by the organization's governing documents or applicable federal or state law.

16. Adopt, codify, and adhere to sound governance processes and meeting procedures; ensure that minutes of the governing body are complete and accurate.

17. Ensure that any governing body policies, procedures, or instructions are committed to writing and, upon adoption, are enforced.

18. Ensure, through the CEO, that the staff of the organization faithfully adheres to the policies and decisions of the governing body.

19. Adopt and enforce a conflict of interest policy, including within it a definition of conflict of interest on the part of the governing body and the method of monitoring compliance with the policy.

20. As individuals, each member of the governing body shall:

    - Refrain from engaging in personal activities that may injure or take advantage of the organization or from using their positions of trust and confidence to further their private interests.

    - Identify, and disclose conflicting or potentially conflicting interest, and decline to participate in a decision where conflict of interest can be alleged.

    - Attend and participate productively and conscientiously in all meetings and be fully acquainted with the bylaws, statements of policy and procedure, and any other governing documents.

continued from page 67

Figure 5.3. Use of Board Development or Training Resources

In the past two years, did your board employ any of the following board development or training resources?	All respondents	Professional societies
Formal orientation for new board members	55%	62%
Board manual	51%	56%
Trainer, speaker, facilitator or consultant hired by the organization to assist with board development	30%	36%
Professional development for the CEO in good governance or board support	30%	40%
Webpage or other electronic resource for board use	28%	42%
Officer succession planning or other means of preparing/ grooming board officers	29%	32%
Annual board member retreat if used for training and not just planning	18%	20%
Mentoring system that matches new and experienced board members	14%	17%

Quite remarkably, occupational and professional societies were considerably more likely than any other organizational type—and ASAE members more likely than nonmembers—to employ individual or multiple means of board training and support (Figure 5.3). What explains the difference? It's premature to conclude the difference rests in ASAE membership, but we note that ASAE does offer regular and consistent messages and training about good governance in its membership resources. Also of interest is that despite their greater expectations for board performance, 501(c)(3) charities were only slightly more likely than other tax statuses to use board development tools.

How often do boards assess their own performance?

While the results above suggest that most boards engaged in some good governance training and development, board members were much less likely to be assessing their own performance. As Figure 5.4 displays, half of the boards of member-serving organizations (52 percent) are not assessing board performance, with little variation

Figure 5.4. Board Self-Evaluation Process

In the past two years, what processes did the board use to evaluate its own performance? (multiple choice)	Frequency
The board did not evaluate its own performance	52%
Informal discussion	25%
Another self-assessment tool designed for our own use	17%
The BoardSource self-assessment tool for associations	4%
Another outside tool	0.9%
The BoardSource self-assessment tool for charities	0.9%
Independent Sector's Principles for Good Governance and Ethical Practice	0.8%

Figure 5.5. Goals Used for Board Self-Assessments

What goals did the board use to evaluate its own performance? (multiple choice, only responses from the one half of organizations employing board self-assessment are included)	Frequency
The board did not set any performance goals for itself	55%
Attendance at board or committee meetings	23%
Giving or fundraising	13%
Membership recruitment	12%
Advocacy or political engagement	12%
Community or membership outreach	10%
Nominating others for board or committee service	8%
Performance on strategic or business plan	3%
Other	2%

among organizational types. Of those which do, the most common performance targets they assess are attendance, giving, fundraising, and membership recruitment (Figure 5.5). The reader should note that we cannot distinguish assessments of the board as a whole from individual board member assessments.

The majority of those who self-assess do it through informal discussion and do not use a formal tool or process. When used, most tools are homegrown. This is not necessarily a bad thing: Reliance on self-developed tools could be beneficial since each organization can shape the process to meet its unique goals (Lichtsteiner and Lutz, 2012).

However, these results also suggest that the majority of boards of directors are not availing themselves of the myriad number of professionally developed self-assessment tools that are now available to boards of directors. Even those tools with high name recognition, such as BoardSource's self-assessment tools, are in surprisingly small use. BoardSource offers two separate versions developed for charities and associations (the latter in cooperation with ASAE). Not surprisingly, professional and occupational societies were much more likely to be using the BoardSource tool for associations compared to other organizational types, but even so, the rate of use was just 6.4 percent (3.3 percent for trade associations). Of the standardized tools in use, in addition to those specified in the survey, CEOs mentioned the Carver Policy Governance model, other standards from their fields (e.g., the Museum Assessment Program, or a tool for YMCAs), the "7 Measures of Success" processes, self-designed surveys, and tools brought by consultants.

Several CEOs described ad hoc methods of board self-assessment, such as "plus/delta" reviews of each board meeting. Many observed that board members assessed their own performance against the organization's business plan and strategic objectives. Assessment of performance against the business plan would help in meeting strategic objectives, but would not substitute for a process focused on effective governance.

Staff support of the board: Is more better?

The literature on good governance refers frequently to the value of a strong relationship between board members and staff. What has not been explored in prior research is the question of how much staff time should be spent supporting board members? Is more staff support always better, or could more hours signal a weak board that staff are shoring up?

The literature on good governance refers frequently to the value of a strong relationship between board members and staff. What has not been explored in prior research is the question of how much staff time should be spent supporting board members?

We asked CEOs and executive directors to tell us, to the best of their recollection, how much total time they spent personally managing and supporting the board and its committees. We asked them to do this for themselves, and also to estimate the time other staff members spent in activities such as preparing board and committee materials, communicating with board members, planning and staffing board and committee meetings, documenting decisions, and similar activities.

Among CEOs, 11 percent of respondents spent one hour or less per week supporting their board, and 50 percent spent five or fewer hours per week. In addition to CEO time, one quarter of member-serving organizations spend one or fewer staff hours per week, and 50 percent spend five hours or less. Cumulatively, this averages to 12 hours per week of staff time, or the equivalent of one quarter FTE staff support for the board. The results displayed in Figure 5.6 suggest a fairly even distribution of hours from just one to two per week up to the equivalent of a full FTE in staff time.

Contrary to what one might assume, the number of staff hours spent supporting the board was only minimally correlated with the overall number of staff in the organization (0.100, $p < 0.01$), and not related at all to board size, budget size, or number of board meetings. This result indicates that board staffing is intentional, driven not only by organizational capacity but also the objective of a strong board. For example, we found that staff time spent on board support decreased the number of reported board problems, such as the absence of a quorum at a meeting or the early departure of a board member. We also found that as staff time increased, the amount of board development activity increased. These results suggest a strong return on investment for staff support of the board.

Figure 5.6. CEO and Staff Time Spent Supporting the Board

How much total time (in average hours or days per week or month) do you as CEO or other staff members spend personally managing and supporting the board and its committees? (in deciles)		0%	100%
0–2 hours/week	7%		
3–5 hours/week	13%		
6–7 hours/week	9%		
8–9 hours/week	10%		
10–11 hours/week	8%		
12–15 hours/week	12%		
16–19 hours/week	9%		
20–25 hours/week	12%		
26–39 hours/week	10%		
40 or more hours/week	10%		

CHAPTER SIX

How Do CEOs Rate Their Board's Performance?

THIS CHAPTER PULLS TOGETHER the governance practices explored so far to test their effects on CEO assessments of board performance. The central proposition tested in this chapter is that board performance depends on a variety of organizational circumstances, both external to the organization and internally driven by good governance practices. This chapter has two sections: a summary of CEOs ratings on 20 measures of board performance and an exploration of the characteristics that seem to have the strongest connection to high-performing boards. We'll discuss the key findings and what they mean throughout this chapter.

In this chapter, the voice of the CEO is front and center. Many studies rely on CEOs and executive directors to assess board performance. The practice is more than merely efficient; staff can provide a more objective view than board members might offer when asked to assess themselves. But staff assessments of boards can also be biased, shaped by staffmembers' own opinions and how much they have at stake in their answers.

KEY FINDINGS

- According to CEOs, boards generally do well at meeting their internal accountability and stewardship responsibilities.

- Boards do worst at setting and enforcing performance standards for themselves.

- CEOs also suggest that boards need to improve their advocacy and external relations with chapters, members, and other key stakeholders.

- Board training and self-assessment are productive, with the choice of self-assessment tool much less important than the decision to commit to the process itself.

- CEOs value boards with a strategic orientation, characterized by ongoing, strategic thinking and discussion.

- Not at all surprisingly, high performing boards depend not only on internal board processes but also on the strength of the organization as well as the quality, experience and perspectives of the CEO and staff.

We rely on CEO opinions here because we also wish to understand how their own experience shapes their answers. For example, *7 Measures of Success* (ASAE 2006; revised edition, 2012) challenged the conventional wisdom that CEOs are more effective when they are association professionals who come from outside the organization and its membership. Because we included staff characteristics in our survey, we have an opportunity here not only to test this proposition but also to understand how other CEO characteristics (training, experience, tenure) shape their assessments of board performance.

The performance measures

The measures of board effectiveness tested here were drawn from many sources. Although not all have been used in research before, they represent much of the collective wisdom on board expectations. For example, *7 Measures of Success* (ASAE 2006; revised edition, 2012) observes the value in a board that engages its membership vigorously, taking every advantage to communicate with stakeholder groups. In addition, some CEOs who helped us develop this study through cognitive interviews and survey pretesting steered us toward what they considered to be the primary goal of a good board: a strong strategic focus.

The governance literature identifies many additional board expectations: that they assume legal accountability for their actions (Green and Griesinger, 2006), achieve strong interpersonal relations with stakeholders (Chait, Holland, and Taylor, 1991), avoid destructive interpersonal conflicts with staff or among themselves (Bradshaw, Murray, and Wolpin, 1992), and manage their fiduciary duties effectively (Miller, 2002). Those familiar with the Balanced Scorecard performance model will also recognize the value in an environment that fosters learning and growth (Kaplan, 2003). Board members contribute to this environment by developing their strategic knowledge, and by encouraging open communication and self-evaluation. Although we do not measure secondary effects in this study, boards with these qualities often help achieve additional objectives for organizations, such as the ability to leverage broad stakeholder representation on the board into stronger collaborative performance (Gazley, Chang, and Bingham, 2010). After refinements offered by our survey pretesters, we included 20 measures of board performance in this survey.

CEO assessments of board relations with stakeholders

As displayed in Figure 6.1, CEOs overall found that board members were best at board-staff relations and internal board relations. They were least successful at board-chapter and board-member relations, with nearly one in five suggesting room for improvement. Nearly half of CEOs also thought their boards needed to improve in member outreach (Figure 6.3). Some association experts argue that there's not much ROI for national boards to focus on local chapter issues, but these results suggest that many CEOs don't find their boards effective at chapter relations regardless of what position they take. In the next section of this chapter, we control for organizational characteristics to understand what board practices achieve the best success with member and chapter relations.

Figure 6.1. Quality of Board Relationships with Stakeholders

Considering the past two years, and in your own opinion, please rate the quality of board relations with various stakeholders, using the scale provided.

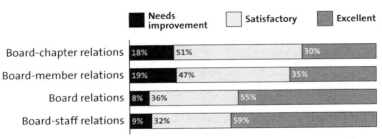

Note: N ranges from 694–1,541 (frequencies omit non-responses and responses of "not applicable").

CEO assessments of board performance

When assessing other measures of board performance, our results find a gap between two groups of performance measures in terms of how effective CEOs think their boards are. We separate these responses into two tables for ease of comparison. Figure 6.2 displays five questions where more than half of CEOs (52 percent to 64 percent) rated their

Figure 6.2. Measurement of Board Performance, Activities Rated Most Positively

Assessing the board as a whole, how would you rate the board's track record with respect to the following activities? (Note that you may select "N/a=not applicable" for those activities your board is not engaged in.)

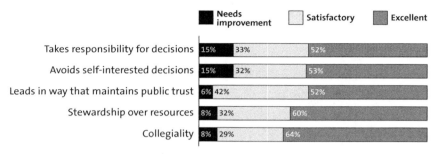

boards excellent. They include board activities related to the board's stewardship and fiduciary duties, such as willingness to take responsibility for decisions, avoiding conflicts of interest, and leading in a way that maintains the public trust in nonprofits.

On the remaining 11 questions, displayed in Figure 6.3, no more than 31 percent of CEOs ranked their boards as excellent on any performance measure. Overall, 23 percent to 69 percent assessed their board as needing improvement in one or more areas. CEOs rated their boards

CEOs rated their boards weakest on setting and enforcing their own performance standards.

weakest on setting and enforcing their own performance standards. Overall, CEOs also considered boards to be lacking in the ability to achieve strategic goals and to be externally oriented.

Figure 6.3. Measurement of Board Performance, Activities That Need Improvement

Assessing the board as a whole, how would you rate the board's track record with respect to the following activities? (Note that you may select "N/a=not applicable" for those activities your board is not engaged in.)

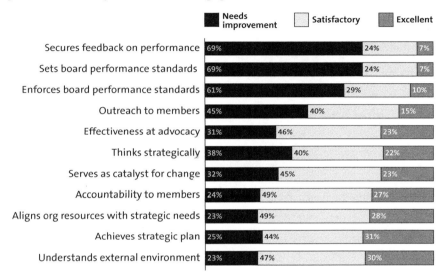

Underlying dimensions of board performance

Because we included such a long list of board performance measures in this study, there is some value in grouping them to understand their relationship to one another. Governance experts observe that board performance rarely occurs on a single dimension, since boards serve a variety of fiduciary, political, strategic, and interpersonal roles (see for example Chait, Holland, and Taylor, 1991).

In the following tables, we organize board performance measures according to the results of a principal components analysis.[1] This method looks for correlations among survey responses and helps to group them thematically. In this instance, we found that CEOs

---

[1] Principal components extraction is based on correlations and employs Varimax rotation, using 70 percent variance explained as the cutoff point.

Figure 6.4. Dimensions of Board Performance

Stewardship
– Overall quality of board relations with staff
– Overall quality of relations among board members
– Stewardship over the organization's resources
– Willingness of the board to take responsibility for difficult decisions
– Ability to make decisions based on organizational interests and not self interest
– Collegiality of the board atmosphere
– Leading the org. in a way that maintains the public trust in nonprofits

Strategic performance
– Effectiveness at strategic rather than operational thinking
– Board participation in advocacy, public policy
– Effectiveness at aligning organization's resources with strategic needs
– Ability to serve as a catalyst for change
– Understanding of organization's external environment and trends
– Ability to achieve strategic plan

Internal accountability
– Board's ability to set performance standards for itself
– Board's record of enforcing self-imposed performance standards
– Securing feedback on its own performance from key constituencies

Member relations
– Overall quality of board relations with the membership
– Accountability to members
– Direct outreach and engagement of membership

Chapter relations
– Overall quality of board-chapter relations (if applicable)

reflected five themes in their expectations of board members. The strongest dimension included seven questions related to the board's stewardship responsibilities, such as an expectation that board members would serve as fiduciaries of the organization's resources, would avoid conflicts of interest, and would lead in a way that maintains the public trust in nonprofits. A second dimension included six questions about the board's strategic performance, including the ability of the board to engage in strategic thinking and serve as a catalyst for change. The third dimension reflects the board's success at holding itself accountable, including through self-assessment and feedback. Fourth, a dimension reflects the board's ability to serve the organization's membership effectively. The final dimension included a single question related to the quality of board-chapter relations (note that not all of the survey participants had a chapter structure).

Accounting for multiple influences on board performance

As we've discussed earlier, and as our conceptual model laid out in Chapter Two, the literature is clear that board performance is contingent on many situational factors, including the type of organization (e.g., tax status, geographic scope, size), the nature of its external environment (e.g., competitive, market growth), and its internal environment (such as stable staffing and management quality). Board performance is also contingent on how effectively a board manages itself. Regression analysis is a statistical approach to understanding how these factors relate to one another. Because organizational performance can sometimes be credited to larger and more resourced organizations, this analytic approach is also very helpful at helping a reader understand patterns of related behaviors within organizations that are intentional and not dependent on size and other measures of organizational capacity.

The following tables use ordinary least squares and logistic regression analysis, using each board performance measure displayed in the left hand column as an outcome of interest (i.e., the dependent variables). In Figure 6.5, we control for tax status. In Figures 6.6 and onward, we also control for certain organizational characteristics (see footnotes). A "plus" sign signals a positive and statistically significant relationship between an organizational characteristic and board

Figure 6.5. Environmental Factors: Board Performance Related to External Dynamics

	Membership growth	Budget growth	More competition for members	International association	Organization age	Budget size
Too much board turnover					−	+
Difficult to find board members	−		−	−	−	+
CEO's total board performance rating	+	+		−		+

HOW TO READ THESE TABLES

These tables are simplified representations of a regression model. They allow us to understand whether the board characteristics listed across the top row (vertical axis) have an influence on a rating of "Excellent" in any of the performance measures listed down the left-hand column (horizontal axis). A plus sign shows positive relationships, a minus sign shows negative relationships. For example, in Figure 6.6, on the first performance measure, "overall quality of board relations with staff," we can conclude that as "board size" increases, CEOs are more likely to rate their boards excellent in terms of the quality of board-staff relations. "Term limits" also increase CEO ratings of excellence in board-staff relations, but boards with "external nominations" and "diversity requirements" are less likely to be rated "excellent" in board-staff relations. In the bottom row, a plus or minus sign indicates a positive or negative relationship between these board characteristics and the board's overall performance rating (calculated by summing up the ratings for all performance metrics).

Each performance measure was analyzed separately, using all of the listed board characteristics plus additional "control variables" that are not displayed but that account for organizational differences (upward growth in budget, growth in membership, staff size, organizational age, budget size, tax status with c-7 and upward as reference, international geographic scope). All relationships displayed are statistically significant.

performance, while a "minus" sign denotes a negative relationship. Where relationships are found, it is premature to conclude all are causal, but they do help us identify the most likely characteristics of high-performing boards.

External environment and board performance

As Figure 6.5 displays, the external environment does play a role in board performance, not only in how hard boards must work to recruit members but also in overall performance rankings by their CEOs. Organizations with bigger budgets are less likely to have challenges finding board members and enjoy higher performing boards overall. But as these organizations age, they appear to lose some ability to find who they need. Organizations in competitive environments and those with an international membership face greater recruitment challenges. CEOs reward the boards that achieve membership growth with higher performance ratings even while they report that it's harder to find board members.

Structural factors and board performance

Figure 6.6 tests the influence of board structure and size on high board performance as measured by CEO ratings. Controlling for the external factors described in Figure 6.5 allows us to isolate these environmental dynamics (results for control variables are not shown). In other words, the question becomes "After accounting for membership growth and other happy or unhappy circumstances of the organizational environment, what other factors related to the board structure itself can explain high board performance?"

Management quality and board performance

Figure 6.7 looks at characteristics of the organization's staff leadership. We focus on three factors: training and experience, the role an executive director or CEO plays on the board, and job satisfaction. The

Figure 6.6. Structural Factors: Board Performance Related to Board Size, Selection, and Structure

	Board size	Appointed members	External nominations	Competitive elections	Screening	Diversity requirements	Term limits
Stewardship							
Overall quality of board relations with staff	+		−			−	+
Overall quality of relations among board members		−			+		+
Stewardship over the organization's resources		−			+		
Takes responsibility for difficult decisions		−			+		
Ability to make decisions based on org'l interests and not self interest		−	−		+		
Collegiality of the board atmosphere		−			+		
Leading in a way that maintains the public trust in nonprofits		−	−		+		
Strategic performance							
Effectiveness at strategic rather than operational thinking					+	+	
Board participation in advocacy, public policy	+			+			
Effectiveness at aligning org's resources with strategic needs			−	+	+		
Ability to serve as a catalyst for change					+		+
Understanding of external environment and trends		−			+		
Ability to achieve strategic plan					+		
Internal accountability							
Board's ability to set performance standards for itself						+	
Enforcing self-imposed performance standards							

continued on next page

continued from previous page

	Board size	Appointed members	External nominations	Competitive elections	Screening	Diversity requirements	Term limits
Securing feedback on performance	+						−
Member relations							
Overall quality of board relations with the membership		−					
Accountability to members				+			
Direct outreach and engagement of membership			−	+			
Chapter relations							
Overall quality of board-chapter relations (if applicable)	+	−					
Overall performance ranking	+	−	−	+	+		

question here is, "After accounting for membership growth and other happy or unhappy circumstances of the organizational environment, what does the CEO do to support high board performance?"

Chief conclusions are the following:

- ASAE membership and CAE credentialing support a CEO's role in small but beneficial ways.

- If one were to face the choice of either hiring someone from the same professional field or industry, or hiring someone trained in association management, we found both CEO skill sets are linked to higher board performance—with a slight advantage to training in association management. Even more important, however, is a CEO's tenure in the position.

- Since CEOs who previously served on the board rate their boards higher on good staff-board relations and board-membership relations, this experience appears to pay off.

continued on page 91

Figure 6.7. Management Quality: Board Performance Related to CEO Characteristics

| | Experience | | | | | | Board role | | Attitude |
	ASAE membership	CAE	From same field	Assoc. professional	Former board member	CEO tenure	CEO presides	Ex officio non-voting	Planning to leave
Stewardship									
Overall quality of board relations with staff	+			+	+	+			–
Overall quality of relations among board members						+	+		–
Stewardship over the organization's resources	+					+	+	–	–
Takes responsibility for difficult decisions				+					–
Ability to make decisions based on org'l interests and not self interest						+			–
Collegiality of the board atmosphere	+	+				+			–
Leading in a way that maintains the public trust in nonprofits						+	+	–	–

continued on next two pages

continued from previous page

	Experience					Board role			Attitude
	ASAE membership	CAE	From same field	Assoc. professional	Former board member	CEO tenure	CEO presides	Ex officio non-voting	Planning to leave
Strategic performance									
Effectiveness at strategic rather than operational thinking			+						
Board participation in advocacy, public policy				+			+		–
Effectiveness at aligning org's resources with strategic needs				+		+	+		–
Ability to serve as a catalyst for change				+				–	–
Understanding of external environment and trends			+	+			+	–	–
Ability to achieve strategic plan	+								–
Internal accountability									
Board's ability to set performance standards for self				+					–
Record of enforcing self-imposed performance standards				+		–			–
Securing feedback on its own performance from key constituencies									–

continued on next page

continued from previous page

	Experience						Board role		Attitude
	ASAE membership	CAE	From same field	Assoc. professional	Former board member	CEO tenure	CEO presides	Ex officio non-voting	Planning to leave
Member relations									
Overall quality of board relations with the membership						+			−
Accountability to members					+	+	+		−
Direct outreach and engagement of membership					+		+		
Chapter relations									
Overall quality of board-chapter relations (if applicable)						+	+		−
Overall performance ranking				+		+	+	−	−

continued from page 87

- Regardless of the fact that this is considered a poor governance practice, it's clear that some CEOs prefer to have a vote on the board and rate their boards higher when they do.
- CEOs who are planning to leave the organization most definitely assign some of their dissatisfaction to the board.

The relationship of staffing capacity to board performance

Figure 6.8 illustrates minor but still important influences on board performance based on how the organization is staffed. There are three key findings:

- A board's performance depends on stable, professional staffing.
- The choice of staffing structure (such as external management) matters less than its stability.
- Boards that are more heavily staffed are not using this staff support to generate higher board performance.

Strategic planning and board performance

Figure 6.9 shows in stark terms how important strategic thinking and planning are to board performance:

- High-performing boards have greater strategic orientation. But boards that expend even a moderate amount of time on strategic thinking and planning perform better than those that do not.
- The benefits to be gained from a more strategic orientation are universal and not just focused on the dimension of board strategic performance.
- A lack of a strategic plan causes more problems for board performance than the choice of whether the plan is staff-led or board-led.

continued on page 95

Figure 6.8. Staff Capacity: Board Performance Related to Staffing Characteristics

	Staff time supporting board	Mgmt. firm	Volunteer staff	Stable staff
Stewardship				
Overall quality of board relations with staff			−	+
Overall quality of relations among board members			−	+
Stewardship over the organization's resources				+
Willingness of the board to take responsibility for difficult decisions				+
Ability to make decisions based on org'l interests and not self interest	−		−	+
Collegiality of the board atmosphere			−	+
Leading in a way that maintains the public trust in nonprofits				+
Strategic performance				
Effectiveness at strategic rather than operational thinking	−			
Board participation in advocacy / public policy				
Effectiveness at aligning org's resources with strategic needs			−	
Ability to serve as a catalyst for change			−	
Understanding of organization's external environment and trends		+		+
Ability to achieve strategic plan		−	−	+
Internal accountability				
Board's ability to set performance standards for itself				+
Board's record of enforcing self-imposed performance standards		+	−	
Securing feedback on its own performance from key constituencies				

continued on next page

continued from previous page

	Staff time supporting board	Mgmt. firm	Volunteer staff	Stable staff
Member relations				
Overall quality of board relations with the membership	−			+
Accountability to members			+	+
Direct outreach and engagement of membership				
Chapter relations				
Overall quality of board-chapter relations (if applicable)				+
Overall performance ranking (added up)			−	+

Figure 6.9. Board Performance and Strategic Orientation

	No strategic plan	Staff-led strategic plan	Joint board-staff plan	High strategic orientation	Moderate strategic orientation
Stewardship					
Overall quality of board relations with staff		+	+	+	+
Overall quality of relations among board members		+	+	+	+
Stewardship over the organization's resources		+	+	+	+
Willingness of the board to take responsibility for difficult decisions				+	+
Ability to make decisions based on org'l interests and not self interest		+	+	+	+
Collegiality of the board atmosphere	+	+	+	+	+
Leading in a way that maintains the public trust in nonprofits			+	+	+

continued on next page

continued from previous page

	No strategic plan	Staff-led strategic plan	Joint board-staff plan	High strategic orientation	Moderate strategic orientation
Strategic performance					
Effectiveness at strategic rather than operational thinking	−			+	+
Board participation in advocacy / public policy				+	+
Effectiveness at aligning org's resources with strategic needs	−			+	+
Ability to serve as a catalyst for change	−		+	+	+
Understanding of organization's external environment and trends	−			+	+
Ability to achieve strategic plan	−			+	+
Internal accountability					
Board's ability to set performance standards for itself	−		+	+	+
Board's record of enforcing self-imposed performance standards	−		+	+	+
Securing feedback on its own performance from key constituencies				+	+
Member relations					
Overall quality of board relations with the membership		+		+	+
Accountability to members				+	+
Direct outreach and engagement of membership	−			+	+
Chapter relations					
Overall quality of board-chapter relations (if applicable)		+		+	+
Overall performance ranking (added up)		+	+	+	+

continued from page 91

• Strategic thinking and discussion are as important as a strategic plan.

The board and a culture of learning

In Figure 6.10, we look at the value of board self-assessment and board development activities. We find that:

• CEOs will rate boards more poorly on internal accountability if those boards do not assess their own performance.

• Surprisingly, however, many boards that have avoided a self-assessment appear to maintain strong relationships with staff, members, chapters, and among themselves. It may be that some staff or board members rationalize away a self-assessment based on perceived lack of need. However, as our results show, these boards may not be recognizing how a self-assessment can support strategic orientation.

• The choice of self-assessment tool is much less important than the decision to commit to the process itself. In fact, both formal and informal self-assessment activities support board performance.

• Comparing boards that engage in any board development activities with the quantity of activities they employ, we find a strong case for investing in numerous training and development activities.

Figure 6.10. The Board and a Culture of Learning: Board Performance Related to Board Development, Training, and Self-Assessment

	Self assessment		Board development	
	No self assessment	Informal discussion is part of self assessment	Yes—any board development	Total number of board development activities
Stewardship				
Overall quality of board relations with staff	+	+		+
Overall quality of relations among board members	+	+		+
Stewardship over the organization's resources		+		+
Willingness of the board to take responsibility for difficult decisions		+		+
Ability to make decisions based on org'l interests and not self interest		+		+
Collegiality of the board atmosphere	+	+	+	+
Leading in a way that maintains the public trust in nonprofits		+	+	+
Strategic performance				
Effectiveness at strategic rather than operational thinking		+	+	+
Participation in advocacy, public policy		+		+
Effectiveness at aligning org's resources with strategic needs		+		+
Ability to serve as a catalyst for change		+		+
Understanding of organization's external environment and trends		+		
Ability to achieve strategic plan	−		+	+

continued on next page

continued from previous page

	Self assessment		Board development	
	No self assessment	Informal discussion is part of self assessment	Yes—any board development	Total number of board development activities
Internal accountability				
Board's ability to set performance standards for itself	−			
Board's record of enforcing self-imposed performance standards	−			+
Securing feedback on its own performance from key constituencies	−	+		+
Member relations				
Overall quality of board relations with the membership	+	+		+
Accountability to members		+		+
Direct outreach and engagement of membership		+		+
Chapter relations				
Overall quality of board-chapter relations (if applicable)	+	+	−	+
Overall performance ranking	+	+	+	+

KEY FINDINGS RELATED TO A BOARD'S STRUCTURE

- Board size supports performance in minor ways such as improved relations with members and chapters—perhaps by giving board members the greater numbers and capacity to engage these stakeholders.

- The method for selecting board members matters, with external appointments and nominations hampering a board's ability to meet stewardship and fiduciary responsibilities.

- While the leading thought is to avoid competitive elections because they generate winners and losers, our results suggest that competitive elections actually support good board relations with the membership.

- Screening prospective board members for qualifications before electing them is the single most important selection method for building a high-performing board.

- Boards with diversity and representational requirements achieve minor gains in strategic performance and internal accountability, but they also challenge board-staff relations.

- Terms limits also support a strong board, with the only qualification that they may give a board less time to secure feedback on its own performance.

CHAPTER SEVEN

Benchmarking "Good Governance"

ARE BOARDS RESPONDING TO the expectations of members, the public, and regulators for good governance? There is encouraging news in this study but also some cause for concern.

Environment matters: The member-serving sector is large, diverse, and complex. Governance practices reflect this diversity. The competitiveness of an organization's environment, its geographic scope, complexity, and budget dynamics influence a board's ability to recruit the members it needs and secure the stable staffing on which boards depend. Board members who can make the time commitment and those with the necessary skills are in high demand.

Many member-serving boards do practice a culture of learning: Across all tax statuses and organizational missions, albeit with some variance, we find the majority of boards have invested in board training and development through both formal and informal means. Even after controlling for differences in organizational size, complexity, geography, etc., we also find that board development pays off in higher CEO assessments of board performance.

Many boards are actively engaged in meeting fiduciary responsibilities: Although we did not find 100 percent compliance with any recommended practice, the majority of member-serving boards insist on training and development and have forged good relations with staff and other board members. The majority of boards take responsibility for decisions, avoid conflicts of interest, and serve as excellent stewards of organizational resources and the public's trust.

Member-serving boards follow many effective governance practices: Most boards screen prospective board members before electing them, and this practice matters when it comes to performance. So do term limits, competitive elections, and diversity requirements, which play a role not only in healthy board turnover but also contribute to key performance objectives. Most boards appear to be determining their size based more on the pursuit of efficiency than on an organization's representational needs. Many invest in strong committee structures and organize board meeting time to achieve strategic goals.

Strategically oriented boards reap widespread benefits: Many experts have urged boards to become more strategically oriented, but we find here just how valuable such activities can be across a wide range of performance criteria. Not only is there a striking difference in CEO performance ratings for boards that are not engaged in strategic planning compared to those that are, but we also find marginal improvements in ratings when boards actively engage in strategic planning rather than relying on staff-led plans. And we find that even a moderate focus on strategic thinking results in real gains for boards across all of our performance categories, including stewardship, accountability, and external relations.

But some boards are still engaged in problematic practices: Boards relying on non-elected, indirectly appointed members will undoubtedly argue there are representational reasons for this practice but must now acknowledge the harm to board cohesion and high performance. In addition, boards do not yet practice a high level of transparency regarding the makeup of their own membership. Board members sometimes don't show up for the job, causing quorums to fail and creating problematic vacancies. Half of member-serving boards do not yet assess their own performance. Given this state, they were justifiably rated lowest of all by management on setting and enforcing performance standards. Many are too insular and not effective at outreach—and it shows in the poor quality of their chapter and membership relations.

Management matters—but sometimes more than it should: The quality and experience of association leadership matters. Trained association professionals bring skills from which board members also benefit. But boards must recognize that lead staff can ask for more than they should when they expect to preside over boards. And CEOs can also end up in inefficient relationships with boards, providing extra support for boards that are weak performers. Boards must recognize the impact that relying too heavily on staff has on staff morale and performance.

CEOs are voting with their feet: We hope that the strong connection we found between CEO departure plans and low ratings of their boards will serve as sufficient warning to boards that they hold the responsibility not only for their own performance but for a good part of staff job satisfaction. A weak board is a drag on staff, making staff work harder.

Looking forward and making use of this information

For the organizations that feel they are well on the way to surmounting these challenges and achieving good governance, our results will help them by confirming the recipe for a high-performing board:

- A strong strategic orientation and culture

- Effective selection and decision-making procedures

- A culture of learning and assessment

- Close relationships with staff and with one another

Whether you feel your association is on its way to high performance or already there, we suggest this book be used as a starting point for a conversation among chief staff and board members. For those organizations not yet actively engaged in setting and measuring board performance, we hope this conversation will then lead to some goal-setting. So many planning and assessment tools are available to support good governance, there's no need to list them here, but clearly our study finds that the choice of tool is less important than the board's decision to actively engage in learning and self-evaluation.

This self-assessment should result in a better understanding of how the board can be most effectively structured. Once the board is fairly comfortable with its own processes—or at least headed in the right direction—it should turn its attention to board-staff relations. Obviously, boards don't operate in a vacuum. This study supports that perspective with hard—and perhaps hard-to-accept—evidence that some boards rely on staff much more than they should. Paid staff, like boards, must also be given the tools to succeed. For CEOs, it's clear that much of the solution rests in creating board-staff relations that are both supportive—to minimize staff turnover—and also appropriate in the sense that they reinforce rather than erode public trust in nonprofit member-serving organizations.

Our final word is about intentionality: As noted at the beginning of this study, good governance is not about staffing or any other measure of organizational capacity as much as it is about a board's willingness to take its role seriously. A high-functioning board may not have all of the answers, but it's willing to invest in learning them—and to asking good questions about its role along the way. From this perspective, the journey can be as important as the destination.

Methodology

Data come from an electronic survey of 1,585 U.S.-based member-serving organizations. Respondents are the chief staff officers (such as Executive Directors or CEOs for staffed organizations, or board presidents for voluntary organizations). The sample was drawn from two data sources: (1) 3,867 ASAE members, meaning any organization categorized as an association and for which the CEO is a member of ASAE, and (2) 9,524 member-serving organizations that are not ASAE members, drawn in a stratified random sample from a database of 21,326 organizations. This database was created by ASAE, based on IRS 990 returns, and includes any U.S.-based nonprofit organization of any tax status that filed a full form 990 (not an EZ) in 2009 with at least one paid staff member and with some reported revenue from membership (Line VIII.1.b. of the 990 Form).

We employed Datalake Inc., the firm used by the National Center for Charitable Statistics, to collect contact names, emails and addresses for chief staff officers, as well as National Taxonomy of Exempt Entities (NTEE) codes and matching organizational financial and program data from IRS 990 forms. This method failed to produce an email address for approximately 30 percent of our sample. So that response rates are not manipulated, we proceeded with the assumption that these are operating organizations that we just failed to reach, although it is possible that some are not operating.

Therefore, the population sampled represents all U.S. nonprofit organizations of any tax status that indicate on IRS records that they serve a membership, that file a 990 Form, and that employ at least one person. This is a broader definition of "associations" than some employ, but has the advantage of including a range of member-serving organizations, including social clubs, arts organizations, learned societies, trade associations, fraternal associations, sports clubs, and other member-serving groups.

The survey was developed under the guidance of the ASAE Foundation's Governance Task Force, the Indiana University Center for Survey Research, two external governance experts, and the IU Institutional Review Board overseeing human subjects research (IUB Study #1207009078). Following cognitive interviews and a field pretest, the survey was launched November 2012 and closed February 2013. To boost response rates, nonprofit CEOs received five advance or reminder emails, were given immediate access to a summary of responses to date when they completed the survey, and were promised an executive summary of the results following publication. A reminder postal letter was also sent to selected non-respondents in order to increase the response rate among subgroups of the sample, such as small organizations.

The final response rate was 12 percent, based on 1,585 valid responses from a sample of 13,304 eligible organizations (i.e., that file independently within the U.S. and are not subsidiaries of another organization). Largely incomplete surveys were removed before calculating this figure. This is a conservative estimate of the response rate, as we note that contact information was available for only 70 percent of our sample. Based on the number of CEOs we were able to contact, the response rate for organizations we reached is 16 percent.

To support reliability and validity of the results, the study used stratified random sampling of the non-ASAE member organizations based on tax status, expenditures, census region, and NTEE professional association classification. The analysis weights non-ASAE member cases on these characteristics so that the final group of responding organizations mirrors the original sample. For organizations represented in ASAE membership, the final group of respondents were weighted to closely reflect all ASAE members' characteristics on organization type (trade association, professional association, combined professional/trade-mainly individuals, combined trade/professional-mainly company), income, and census region. Weighting allows a researcher with sufficient information about the original population being sampled to match the responding cases to the full population. This method allows small datasets to produce generalizable results assuming that these organizational characteristics are highly correlated with the characteristics of interest in a governance study. Under this assumption, the results represent U.S. member-serving associations with an overall margin of error of 2–3 percent (margins of error will be larger for the few survey questions only asked of a subgroup of respondents and when analyzing specific types of organizations separately, such as 501(c)(3) organizations, occupational or professional societies, and international organizations).

Of the survey respondents, one-quarter had served as the chief staff officer of the organization for three years or less, and a further one-quarter had served for up to six years. Twenty-one percent of respondents held a Certified Association Executive (CAE) credential, and 12 percent held another association management credential. Thirty-seven percent were trained as association professionals, and 52 percent were trained in the field their organization serves (14 percent described themselves as both trained association professionals and representative of their field). Ninety-five percent of respondents were in paid staff positions; the remainder identified as volunteers. Slightly more than half (53 percent) were ASAE members.

The ASAE Foundation's Research Committee provided oversight to the survey design, and also participated in reading drafts of the study report and suggesting edits.

About the Authors

Beth Gazley (bgazley@indiana.edu) is associate professor of public affairs and philanthropic studies at Indiana University-Bloomington. Full biography at http://www.indiana.edu/~spea/faculty/gazley-beth.shtml.

Ashley Bowers (afbowers@indiana.edu) is director of the Indiana University Center for Survey Research, and clinical assistant professor in the School of Public and Environmental Affairs. Full biography at http://www.indiana. edu/~spea/faculty/bowers_ashley.shtml.

Contributions to the ASAE Foundation made this research possible.

Bibliography

ASAE: The Center for Association Leadership. 2006, 2012. *7 Measures of Success: What Remarkable Associations Do that Others Don't.* Washington, DC: ASAE: The Center for Association Leadership.

Association Forum of Chicagoland. October 1, 2011. "Association Strategic Governance." From the web at www.associationforum.org.

Association Forum of Chicagoland. March 2012. "Fiduciary and Management Duties for the Association Executive and Governing Body." From the web at www.associationforum.org.

BoardSource. 2012a. *The Nonprofit Answer Book, 3rd ed.* San Francisco: Jossey-Bass.

BoardSource. 2012b. Nonprofit Governance Index 2012: CEO Survey of BoardSource Members. Washington, DC: BoardSource.

BoardSource. 2010a. *The Handbook of Nonprofit Governance.* San Francisco: Jossey-Bass.

BoardSource. 2010b. *BoardSource Nonprofit Governance Index.* Washington, DC: BoardSource.

Bradshaw, Pat, Murray, Vic, and Wolpin, Jacob. 1992. Do Nonprofit Boards Make a Difference? An Exploration of the Relationships Among Board Structure, Process, and Effectiveness. *Nonprofit and Voluntary Sector Quarterly,* 21(3):227–249.

Brown, William A. Board Development Practices and Competent Board Members: Implications for Performance. *Nonprofit Management and Leadership,* 17(3):301–317.

Brown, William A. Inclusive Governance Practices in Nonprofit Organizations and Implications for Practice. *Nonprofit Management and Leadership,* 12(4):369–385.

Carver, John. 1997. *Boards That Make a Difference, 2nd ed.* San Francisco: Jossey-Bass.

Chait, Richard P., Holland, Thomas P., and Taylor, Barbara E. 1991. *The Effective Board of Trustees.* New York: Macmillan.

Chait, Richard C. Holland, Thomas P., and Taylor, Barbara E. 1996. *Improving the Performance of Governing Boards.* Phoenix, AZ: Oryx Press.

Chait, Richard C., Ryan, William P., and Taylor, Barbara E. 2005. *Governance as Leadership: Reframing the Work of Nonprofit Boards.* Washington, DC: BoardSource.

Cornelius, Marla, Rick Moyers, and Jeanne Bell. 2011. *Daring to Lead 2011: A National Study of Nonprofit Executive Leadership.* San Francisco, CA: CompassPoint Nonprofit Services and the Meyer Foundation.

Cornforth, Christopher. 2011. Nonprofit Governance Research: Limitations of the Focus on Boards and Suggestions for New Directions. *Nonprofit and Voluntary Sector Quarterly,* 41(6):1116–1135.

Dignam, Monica and Tenuta, Rosemary. 2013. *Assessing Board Performance: An Analysis of ASAE-BoardSource Board Self-Assessment Results.* Washington, DC: ASAE Foundation.

Engle, Mark. 2013. "The Strategic Decision-Making Process of the Board and Its Impact on Decision Outcomes." Unpublished doctoral thesis, Case Western Reserve University.

Erhardt, Niclas L., Werbel, James D. and Shrader, Charles B. 2003. Board of Director Diversity and Firm Financial Performance. *Corporate Governance,* 11(2):102–111.

Gazley, Beth, Chang, Won Kyung, and Bingham, Lisa Blomgren. 2010. Board Diversity, Stakeholder Representation and Collaborative Performance in Community Mediation Centers. *Public Administration Review,* 70(4):610–620.

Green, Jack C. and Griesinger, Donald W. 2006. Board Performance and Organizational Effectiveness in Nonprofit Social Services Organizations. *Nonprofit Management and Leadership,* 6(4):381–402.

Haynes, Wendy and Gazley, Beth. 2011. Professional Associations and Public Service: Do Associations Matter? In *The State of Public Administration: Issues, Problems, Challenges,* Donald Menzel and Harvey White (eds.). Armonk, NY: M.E. Sharpe.

Herman, Robert and Renz, David O. 1999. Theses on Organizational Effectiveness. *Nonprofit and Voluntary Sector Quarterly,* 28(2):107–126.

Herman, Robert and Renz, David O. 2008. Advancing Organizational Effectiveness Research and Theory: Nine theses. *Nonprofit Management and Leadership,* 18(4):399–415.

Holland, Thomas P. and Jackson, Douglas K. 1998. Strengthening Board Performance. *Nonprofit Management and Leadership,* 9(2):121–134.

Kaplan, Robert S. 2003. Strategic Performance Measurement and Management in Nonprofit Organizations. *Nonprofit Management and Leadership,* 11(3):353–370.

Lakey, Berit, M., Hughes, Sandra R., and Flynn, Outi. 2004. *Governance Committee.* Washington, DC: BoardSource.

Laughlin, Fredric L., and Andringa, Robert C. 2007. *Good Governance for Nonprofits: Developing Principles and Policies for an Effective Board.* New York, NY: American Management Association.

Lichtsteiner, Hans, and Lutz, Vanessa. 2012. Use of Self-Assessment by Nonprofit Organization Boards: The Swiss Case. *Nonprofit Management and Leadership,* 22(4):483–506.

Lipman, Frederick D., and Lipman, L. Keith. 2006. *Corporate Governance Practices: Strategies for Public, Private, and Not-for-profit Organizations.* Hoboken, NJ: Wiley.

Miller, Judith L. 2002. The board as a monitor of organizational activity: The Applicability of Agency Theory to Nonprofit Boards. *Nonprofit Management and Leadership,* 12(4):429–450.

Miller-Millesen, Judith L. 2003. Understanding the Behavior of Nonprofit Boards of Directors: A Theory-Based Approach. *Nonprofit and Voluntary Sector Quarterly,* 32(4):521–547.

Ostrower, Francie. 2007. *Nonprofit Governance in the United States: Findings on Performance and Accountability from the First National Representative Study.* Washington, DC: Urban Institute.

Ostrower, Francie and Stone, Melissa M. 2010. Moving Governance Research Forward: A Contingency-Based Framework and Data Application. *Nonprofit and Voluntary Sector Quarterly,* 39(5):901–924.

Panel on the Nonprofit Sector. 2007. *Principles for Good Governance and Ethical Practice.* Washington, DC: Independent Sector. Available online at http://independentsector.org/principles_guide_summary.

Renz, David O. January 1, 2013. Reframing Governance II. *Nonprofit Quarterly.* Online at http://www.nonprofitquarterly.org/governancevoice/21572-reframing-governance-2.html.

Rominiecki, Joe. January 2013. "Big or Small: What's the Right Size for an Association Board?" *Associations Now.* Washington, DC: ASAE Center.

Tecker, Glenn H., Franckel, Jean S., and Meyer, Paul D. 2002. *The Will to Govern Well.* Washington, DC: American Society of Association Executives.

Tesdahl, D. Benson. 2010. *Better Bylaws: Creating Effective Rules for Your Nonprofit Board, 2nd ed.* Washington, DC: BoardSource.

Van Puyvelde, Stijn, Caers, Ralf, Du Bois, Cind, and Jegers, Marc. 2012. The Governance of Nonprofit Organizations: Integrating Agency Theory with Stakeholder and Stewardship Theories. *Nonprofit and Voluntary Sector Quarterly,* 41(3):431–451.

Von Schnurbein, Georg. 2009. Patterns of Governance Structures in Trade Associations and Unions. *Nonprofit Management and Leadership,* 20(1):97–115.